ANCIENT JUDAISM
AND
THE NEW TESTAMENT

The Economic Background of the Gospels
New Horizons of the Christian Faith
The Growth of the Gospels
Form Criticism: A New Method of New Testament Research
The Beginnings of Our Religion
Frontiers of Christian Thinking
Can we Still Believe in Immortality?
The Idea of a Theological College
The Gospel of the Kingdom
The Practice of Religion
The Earliest Gospel
An Introduction to New Testament Thought
How to Read the Bible
The Gospels, Their Origin and Their Growth
Hellenistic Religions: The Age of Syncretism
Ancient Roman Religion
Early Christianity: collected papers of Burton Scott Easton (edited)
Basic Christian Beliefs
New edition of Edwin Hatch, The Influence of Greek Ideas on Christianity
Commentary on Mark in The Interpreter's Bible
Harper's Annotated Bible: Matthew, Mark, John, Hebrews
The Way of Peace
Christ's Victory and Ours
The Passion of the King
Translation of Johannes Weiss, Primitive Christianity
Translation of Martin Dibelius, The Message of Jesus Christ
Translation of Martin Dibelius, Jesus
The Life and Times of Jesus
The Early Days of Christianity

ANCIENT JUDAISM
AND
THE NEW TESTAMENT

FREDERICK C. GRANT

OLIVER AND BOYD
EDINBURGH AND LONDON
1960

OLIVER & BOYD LTD
Tweeddale Court
Edinburgh 1

39a Welbeck Street
London W.1

First Published (New York) . . 1959
Second Edition 1960

Contents

Part Four: THE PRESENT OUTLOOK

Foreword

The Christian Church is heir to an immense and most distant past. No institution in the world maintains its primitive inheritance more tenaciously. This is obviously one source of its strength. But the manner in which it claims and retains its inheritance may also be a source of weakness. This is conspicuously true of its inheritance from ancient Judaism. How shall we appraise this element in its legacy? And how are we to interpret the use which the church has made of it? Are there values still to be discovered in it, beyond those found hitherto? Some persons deny outright the value of this inheritance; others even deny its existence. Many regret that the church obligated itself in any degree to Judaism, viewing this obligation as a handicap; and the less said of it the better. But all such views fly in the face of the plain, obvious facts of history, and twist the documentary evidence out of all recognition. The simple, unmistakable, undeniable fact is that Christianity originated as a movement within the ancient Jewish religion, and that it goes back to the life, teaching, death and resurrection of a Jewish prophet, Jesus of Nazareth.

It is obvious that the Christian religion began as a messianic movement within first century Palestinian Judaism. It is probably a mistake to describe it as a "sect", like the sects of the Pharisees, the Sadducees, and the Essenes—for these were really parties within Judaism, not independent movements. But the Christians, or Nazarenes, as they were called, came nearer to being an independent group, from the very outset, than did any other group within first century Judaism; for them separation was only a matter of time. From the very outset, according to the New Testament, their leaders criticised, or at least questioned, several of the cardinal, fundamental principles of the Jewish religion, such as the permanence and divine authority of the Mosaic Law, the validity and permanence of the temple worship, the meaning and value of sacrifice. It is true that the same criticisms had been voiced by more than one Old Testament prophet; but the difference now lay in the total point of view. The ultimate loyalty of the Christians was not to Judaism but to the new and, they believed, higher revelation of the will of God which at many points now superseded the traditional code, cultus, and beliefs. They not only called in question, or even flatly rejected, the scribal interpretation of the Law; they also rejected the provisions of the Law itself, being led to take this step by the example and the explicit statements of Jesus. At the same time the fundamental presuppositions of the earliest Christian teachers, writers, and thinkers continued to be mainly those of the traditional, contemporary Jewish religion: monotheism, divine revelation, the eschatological view of history. There is only one God, and he has revealed himself to mankind, as the Jewish scriptures say; we are not left to blind "feeling after him, if haply we may find him", for he has declared himself, his purposes and his requirements, and our human duty consists in obedient response to his revelation. God is in control of history, as the scriptures also say, and he is "working his purpose out" toward the final goal of his creation. The world is God's creation, and he will not abandon it to its present state of frustration and defeat, engulfed in human and demonic sin and disobedience and consequent relapse into semi-chaos. The One who created the world and "saw all things" and pronounced them "very good" will not, cannot, sit idly by—or above—the wreckage, and admit the failure of his plans and purposes.

The whole eschatological view of history, which was characteristic of Judaism, as against all Oriental theories of illusion and Greek theories of cyclic repetition, means that God will eventually bring order out of chaos, victory out of defeat, the final achievement of his purposes out of their temporary frustration. Thus the hope of resurrection, judgment, restoration, and "the life of the world to come" is an indispensable element in Judaism. As in the Old Testament, it was the fundamental Jewish belief—shared even by those who minimised eschatology—that the one true God who created heaven and earth still sits enthroned above it; his purpose "ruleth over all"; he still, as on the day of the primal creation, "sits above the water-flood [the primeval chaos] and remains a king for ever". These ideas are as fundamental, as indispensable, and as dear to Christians as they are to Jews. That they were fundamental to the early Christians is clear not only from Paul's letters, the oldest Christian writings we possess, but also from the earliest sources underlying the gospels, from the Book of Acts, and from the early Christian literature (outside the New Testament) surviving from the first four centuries.

The entire New Testament, though written in Greek, has a Jewish orientation, and can be understood only in relation to its Jewish background and antecedents, whether in Palestine or in the Western Diaspora, or in both. The religious thought or "theology" of the New Testament is really a body of Jewish religious thought—even the specifically Christian element is basically Jewish in outlook, terminology, and conception—which is in process of transition, moving in the direction of the doctrinal formulations of the early Catholic church. This movement is like the slow but inevitable rotation of an iceberg or a planet whose centre of gravity has altered and whose axis is consequently shifting. The old double centre, the Torah (revelation) and its implied Covenant, or the Covenant and its consequent Torah (viewed as Law), has now been replaced by a new double centre, namely, Christ and his Church—the Messiah who has finally arrived in the person of Jesus of Nazareth and is soon to "appear" or to "come again" as the messianic judge, and the messianic community of his followers, his "elect", his "saints". Jesus' revelation of God, his interpretation of the will, the nature, the character, the purposes and the requirements of God, forms the basis of the new *halakah* of the Christians—not a revelation of the nature of God in metaphysical terms, but only his purposes and requirements.

Yet it does not repudiate but completes and fulfills the older revelation. So Matthew maintains (see Matt. v.17-20), and so does the old Palestinian tradition underlying the other gospels. Paul goes further: as he implies, in his Letter to the Galatians, the traditional mother-faith, Judaism, had been in reality an ethnic religion—one of the many ethnic or national cults which had come down from antiquity or even from pre-history; while the new daughter-faith (the "gospel", as he usually preferred to call it) was, as he says elsewhere, the final revelation of the "mystery", the plan which all along had been "hidden" in the mind of God; it represented his gracious purpose of salvation and of good for all mankind. Paul's view sounds very "advanced", almost Gnostic. But the thought and even the language of this explanation of the new and final chapter in the story of salvation, this *Heilsgeschichte*, are taken from the older faith, chiefly from the Bible, our Old Testament. And Paul, the Jewish Hellenist, using the Greek translation of the Hebrew scriptures, does not attempt to describe the new revelation in any other terms—as for example in popular philosophical or ethical or mystery cult language, or in Persian or Egyptian terms, some of which were now becoming well known in the Mediterranean world under the early empire. In fact it is inconceivable that such an attempt should have been made, in the first century, by anyone whose native roots were nourished in the soil of Judaism. What later minds undertook—men like the Gnostics, or Celsus, or Alexander Severus, or the emperor Julian—only shows how totally impossible and foredoomed to failure was such a non-Jewish amalgam.

It is the purpose of this book to show that the relations between the New Testament and ancient Judaism, that is, between the early Christian church, its hopes, beliefs, and practices, above all its worship, and the mother-faith, are such that one cannot truly understand the New Testament or the religion it enshrines without a deep and sympathetic understanding of Judaism. As Pope Pius said, in defending the victims of Fascist persecution, "We Christians are also Jews". By the same token, a blind spot for Judaism and its religious values will leave one blind to the deepest meaning of the New Testament and the religion it sets forth. It may be that this will be viewed as a new and radical interpretation of the New Testament and of early Christian history—and the present book a revolutionary manifesto. But it is only an attempt to bring together the results of modern research in order to correct the distortion which centuries of anti-Jewish prejudice have produced in biblical studies. This correction is long overdue, and we are beginning to see that "anti-Semitic" prejudice has obscured the full meaning of the New Testament and of the Christian faith from the earliest period of its history. For a true interpretation of the gospel, of the church itself, of the early Christian ethics and theology, what is called the ancient Jewish "element" must be more positively recognised and appraised: it is really a substratum rather than an element. This challenge is the subject of Chapters I and II. The unique and distinctive features in Christianity are not to be overlooked. In fact they become more distinct when the two strands of Judaism and Graeco-Roman Hellenism are more sharply distinguished; and to ignore the positive values in ancient Judaism only beclouds the issue. Early Christianity was no Gentile, ethnic, philosophical movement, but a movement of messianic enthusiasm originating in the heart of the Jewish homeland. Nor was early Christianity a theological system, but a religion of piety and observance, faith and hope, centred in the scriptures and in the "new life in Christ". It was a new "way of life" which went beyond the traditional scribal or rabbinic interpretation of the Bible, and produced additional new scriptures, a new worship, a new devotion and piety.

All this stands out even more clearly when we study the early church and its doctrines, its faith and its "ways" against the background of contemporary Judaism. The contacts, and the common elements, and also the contrasts and divergences, become clear only when we examine carefully the actual belief and practice of ancient Judaism. This is undertaken, briefly, in Chapters III to VI, where the central emphases of Judaism are studied in relation to the new post-exilic institution, the synagogue, its liturgy—continuous with the Old Testament in thought and aspiration—its emphasis on prayer and study and good works (Ch. III), and the fundamental doctrines, that is, teachings, which it presupposed. Without possessing either a dogmatic creed or a confessional affirmation, or theological formulae of any kind beyond the simple affirmations derived from the scriptures, it held that God is One, that he is the Creator, that he has revealed himself, that he loves mankind, that he chose Israel to be his servant and emissary, that he established the divine Covenant under which he accepts the sacrifices, offerings, and gifts of men, that he punishes sin and wickedness but forgives the penitent, that he will establish his perfect Reign "at the end of days" and will raise up the righteous and those who have died as martyrs in his cause to enjoy eternal bliss in the Age to Come (Chs. iv-v). Since all biblical religion is "eschatological", that is, concerned with the end or goal of God's realised purposes, the distinctive element in "apocalyptic", a new type of religious thought which succeeded and supplanted prophecy during the three centuries between 200 B.C. and A.D. 100, must be recognised and clearly characterised (Ch. vi). Although both prophecy and apocalyptic are represented in the New Testament, and although Jesus himself was a prophet rather than an apoca- lyptist, it was the apocalyptic type of thought which became predominant in early Christianity, and crowded out the other, with consequences which have survived to this day. It is a common mistake to assume that, in the first century, apoca- lyptic eschatology was characteristic of Palestinian Judaism as a whole. This view must be corrected before a true appraisal of the relations between Christianity and Judaism, either then or now, can be made.

It is against this background of traditional Jewish faith and piety that the New Testament must be studied. Too often, Judaism has been treated as merely a foil, with the intention of showing the superiority of Christianity; the result has been that every shadow was painted black, every bright light dimmed, and only a caricature of that living religion survived in the imagination of most readers. Unfortunately, the tendency to misrepresent Judaism had already begun before the New Testament itself was complete. But the historical study of the New Testament cannot rest content with ancient apologetics or polemics. The indebtedness of Christianity to Judaism is evident on every page—if also the rising antagonism between the first century church and synagogue. A study of the life and teaching of Jesus, his background and heritage, even within his own family (Chs. vii-ix) illustrates this clearly: Jesus was a Jew, a Galilean, a villager—and a subject of Herod Antipas, in the days when the Roman occupation was engaged in an all-out effort to take over the small but important frontier state which occupied the centre of the Roman defensive shield in the East. All this is indispensable for an understanding of Jesus himself, his teaching, his proclamation of the Kingdom

of God, his "ethics" of non-resistance, penitence, and love—
which was as authentically Jewish and biblical an ethic as was
ever formulated by human lips! The rise of Christianity
remains an utter enigma if Jesus himself and his teaching, his
life, his mighty works, resurrection, and glorification are left
out of account. But that is what some modern historians and
theologians try to offer us: the historians start *in vacuo* with
"religious and social conditions", not a person; the theologians
begin with Paul, and the "gospel" means, for them, the seventh
chapter of Romans.

Finally, the inferences from this view begin to come clear
(Chs. x-xi). Christianity is still a "theological"—or rather a
theistic—religion, not (as some affirm) a "Christological". The
great central approach to God, in the New Testament, is
"through Christ", not "to" him. The sovereignty of God,
which is not only acknowledged but also strongly emphasised
in the classical Christian traditions—Catholic, Orthodox,
Anglican, Lutheran, Calvinist, Reformed—is entirely true to
the New Testament. "In Christ God was reconciling the
world to himself" (II Cor. v.19)—this statement holds the
perfect balance. Christian prayers are still offered "through
Jesus Christ our Lord". It is wholly false and perverse to
use such language as "the Christlike God" or "Christ the new
God of the first century Christians"—this is only a revival of
Gnosticism, as the now popular slogan "God was in Christ"
is only a revived fourth century Apollinarianism. The balance
which ancient Judaism—and the New Testament—supply to
our theology is also evident in the interpretation of scripture
as a whole, which is not a book of doctrinal data but the collected records of an ancient religion, with obvious theological
implications but not a collection of dogmatic proof texts.
(Some readers ignore the history of religion, even of biblical
religion, and take the Bible "as it is", turning it into a quarry
of solid terms or ideas for use in constructing a dogmatic
system.) The Bible is primarily the book of the synagogue and
the church; it is the book read at public worship, the book of
instruction, teaching, and inspiration—but not of dogmatic
theology. It is a blunder, which much of the revived "biblical"
theology popular since 1918 has perpetuated, to take the
Bible away from the lectern and anatomise it in the study.

The same is true of the New Testament "ethics", which cannot possibly be viewed as an ethical "system"—as if the Sermon on the Mount were the Christian's *Nicomachean Ethics*, or Paul's exhortations (for example, on marriage) a final formulation of Christian duty. A recent writer has described the letters of Paul as "the Euclid of Christianity"; nothing could have been further from Paul's own view, or from a sound historical view of the New Testament as a whole. It is the life of the Holy Spirit within the church which assures its guidance "into all truth", revealing things new and old, and inspiring authoritative utterance in crises and in new situations. But like Jesus' own teaching, that of the church rests back upon and is continuous with the whole of the "ethical" teaching of the Old Testament and of ancient Judaism. It cannot be attached to or grafted upon any other system—Greek, Stoic, Marxian, or Naturalist. Jesus' "ethics", and Paul's, are not really "ethics" at all, but religious teaching on subjects of morals and manners, as in the Old Testament and in Judaism. It is a purely religious ethic, not systematic, not philosophical, not governed by some great principle like the Mean, or the greatest good of the greatest number, or the duties of the Wise Man, or whatever men choose as a relatively highest good. It is only when we study New Testament "ethics" against the background of the whole of the ethical-religious teaching of the Old Testament and Judaism that we can begin to appraise Christian ethics in their true character and see their true bearing upon the life of the world today. In fact, the New Testament ethics presuppose the whole development of Hebrew, Old Testament, Jewish ethical teaching during the long centuries which preceded the rise of Christianity. The restoration of the Bible to the lectern, and its study as the "teaching book" of the ancient synagogue, and the reintegration of Christian ethics with their Jewish antecedents—the "de-dogmatisation" of Christology and theology—these are matters of vital moment for the modern church, threatened now with annihilation by the surrounding world of dogmatic secularism, Naturalism, and opposition to all forms of belief in the super-natural.

This book has been a long time in the making, and its underlying convictions are the outcome of many years of study. Some parts of it have appeared, in substance, in various lectures and papers, chiefly the Francis Brigham Denio Lectures on the Bible at Bangor Theological Seminary (1958) and the John C. Shaffer Lectures at the Yale Divinity School (1959). For kind permission to reprint material already used in articles, I am indebted to the editor of *Sacral Kingship*, a Supplement to *Numen*, Professor Raffaele Pettazzoni of the University of Rome; the editor of the *Zeitschrift für die alttestamentliche Wissenschaft*, Professor Johannes Hempel of the University of Göttineng; and the editor of the *Anglican Theological Review*, Dean Sherman E. Johnson of the Church Divinity School of the Pacific. And I am profoundly grateful to the Christian Research Foundation for the generous prize which was awarded the manuscript before publication.

The text of this edition has been somewhat amplified. Chapter vii, § 6, Ch. viii, § 4, and Ch. ix are new. A few references have been added to books and articles which develop further the views set forth in the text.

F. C. G.

Part One

THE PRESENT
SITUATION

CHAPTER ONE

Modern Research versus
Ancient Prejudice

For many centuries the relations between Christianity and Judaism have been enveloped in a fog of misunderstanding, misrepresentation, and controversy. Until quite recently, most theological writers have taken a wholly negative view of the parent religion of the Christian church, treating it as merely the foil against which to show the superiority of Christian teaching, and thus widening the gulf which already separated the two faiths. It is an old habit of theological writers to do this: even the most eminent of the church fathers did not hesitate to hold the Jews responsible for the death of Christ, and to explain the fall of Jerusalem in A.D. 70 and the subsequent scattering of the Jewish nation as the divine punishment for this awful deed.

1. *Origin of the Prejudice*

Traces of this attitude can be detected even in the New Testament. It arose, accordingly, at a very early date, and soon coalesced with and reinforced an already existing strain of anti-Semitism in the pagan world. It seems to be a natural tendency of theologians and controversialists, in all religions or religious movements which have separated from an older faith, to attribute malice, bigotry, stupidity, even hypocrisy to the adherents of the abandoned creed. Of course, such unpleasant qualities may exist, though scarcely in every member of the older faith. But the excuse is certainly an

3

insufficient one in the case before us, the separation of the Christian church from the Jewish synagogue. True, the followers of "the Way" (Acts IX.2, XIX.23) probably were "cast out", that is, excommunicated, by their fellow Jews, and in turn brought retaliatory charges against their former co-religionists. In spite of the effort of the author of Luke-Acts to show that the church represented the true Israel, and was therefore entitled to the same religious toleration which the Jews enjoyed,[1] his thesis was ultimately rejected by both Romans and Jews, and was eventually abandoned by the Christians. The arguments of Paul and of the author of the Epistle to Hebrews, which might have been used for more or less the same purpose, were equally unavailing. By the date of the gospels of Matthew and John, and in their areas (Syria and Egypt?), the breach could no longer be closed. In Acts VII.44-53, in the Epistle of Barnabas, chapters II, XIII-XVI, and in other passages in early Christian literature, "the Jews" were described as a stupid, blundering lot, who built their God a temple of wood and stone and offered him animal sacrifice, when all that he asked of them was pure hearts and clean lips! The Old Testament laws were explained as meant only symbolically.

We need not rehearse the long tale of ostracism, persecution, and misrepresentation which followed in later centuries, when the Jews' own books (not only the Old Testament) were quoted against them; when unscrupulous apostates revealed the secret "calumnies" of Christ ostensibly to be found in the Talmud, and ecclesiastical censors blacked out such passages in the Jews' own manuscripts; when clever but unscrupulous controversialists professed to uncover a cryptic Judaism which threatened to destroy Christianity, the church, public decency, and private morals. The world is not yet—even after the defeat of Hitler—free from the poison of anti-Semitism spread by these traitors to religion and human brotherhood.

So vast has been this flood of prejudice and misrepresentation that even now, with good editions and translations of the post-biblical Jewish literature available everywhere, and with the works of honest historians rather than propagandists before

---

[1] See "The Purpose of Acts" by Burton Scott Easton, reprinted in *Early Christianity* (S.C.M., 1955).

us, we continue to hear and to read the most grotesque descriptions of ancient Judaism. It is still common among half-educated and misinformed preachers and writers to represent Judaism in the time of Christ as a decadent and moribund, sterile, mechanical, purely formal and hypocritical religion, with a remote and unknown God who was worshipped by a routine of sacrifices, formal prayers and services, fasting, and "good works" done only for the sake of "merit". As if our Lord or his gospel could be honoured by defaming and degrading the religion in which he was nurtured! No religion is to be measured by its worst examples—only the saints, only the pious and devout can be taken as fair representatives of any faith; and even if the average adherent does not approximate, even distantly, this exceptional standard (and he never does, in any religion), it is not honest to take the saint of one religion and contrast him with the sinner or the pedestrian adherent of another. It is not fair, for example, to contrast the *foi du charbonnier* of a Catholic peasant with the refined theology and piety of some Protestant divine. And yet people make judgments of this sort all the time! As for Judaism, it may be stated at once that no anti-Semite can hope to understand either the origin of Christianity or its earliest theology, that of the New Testament period. Even the terms sometimes used, for all their appearance of objectivity, are false: for example, one common in Germany before the war, *Spät-Judentum* ("late" Judaism), meaning that of the period of the New Testament. Historically viewed, the Judaism of the New Testament period was not late, but early; it is only by comparison with the Old Testament (most of which reflects "Hebraism", not Judaism), and upon the assumption that contemporary Judaism was in *rigor mortis*, that such a term can be used. The Judaism of the Tannaite period (roughly the first two centuries of our era) was characterised by variety, internal tensions, and divergent tendencies (some of which came to nothing); but it was by no means moribund. Its canon of scripture was not fixed until *circa* A.D. 90. Its liturgy was still in process of formation, was still being altered, though the main outlines had already taken firm shape. Its creed—Judaism never has had a creed; let us say its "articles of faith"—came centuries later: in the first century its divergent schools of biblical interpretation were still vigorous. On its fringes existed such extraordinary sects as the Essenes, the Qumrân community, the so-called Damascus Sect, and also such strange ascetics as Josephus' teacher Bannos; while out in the Diaspora, beyond the borders of Palestine, were found curious movements and doctrines, some of which clearly reflected the influence of popular Hellenistic cults, practices, and philosophy. The main core of Jewish faith and practice was identifiable enough; but the existence of such variations proves that no sterile uniformity had overwhelmed the Jewish religion, of the kind assumed by later controversialists and propagandists.

The modern student has the advantage of being able to consult several works of first-class scholarship, which set the Judaism of the New Testament period in a fairer, more honest light. Chief among them is the *opus magnum* of the late George Foot Moore, *Judaism in the First Centuries of the Christian Era: The Age of the Tannaim* (3 vols., 1927-1930), a work universally recognised as belonging to the very first rank in scholarship. Another book of great importance is *Le Judaïsme palestinien au temps de Jésus-Christ* (2 vols., 1935) by Joseph Bonsirven; still others are *Die Religion des Judentums* (3rd ed., 1926) by Wilhelm Bousset, and the *Studies in Pharisaism and the Gospels* (2 vols., 1917, 1924) by Israel Abrahams. Another very important work is the readable, well-annotated *Rabbinic Anthology* (1938) compiled by Claude G. Montefiore. The vast *Kommentar zum Neuen Testament aus Talmud und Midrasch* (1922-1928), compiled by Hermann L. Strack and Paul Billerbeck, is a treasure house of materials for elucidating the New Testament from the Jewish side, though its best use will naturally be made by students already familiar with the ancient Jewish literature; parallels always need not merely to be cited but to be interpreted, evaluated, and criticised. In addition to these works, there are others, in a steadily growing literature of sound historical interpretation and exegesis, freed from the dogmatic presuppositions and prejudices of the older Christian scholarship. One of its chief merits is that it recognises ancient Judaism for what it positively was, not for what it negatively was not, and does not feel obliged to conclude every chapter with some unfavourable comparison with Christianity, Protestant or Catholic.

2. *The Rise of "Normative" Judaism*

It may be suspected that in much modern research into first century Judaism only those elements are stressed which find parallels in the New Testament or in early Christian teaching. Julius Wellhausen's *bon mot* is often quoted: "Everything in the Sermon on the Mount can be found in the Talmud —yes, *and how much else!*" Only a firsthand study of the ancient Jewish sources can clear up the situation. But such a study must not be conducted with prejudice—prejudice against "legalistic" religion, or in favour of "apocalyptic", going the length sometimes of identifying first century Palestinian Judaism not with the Law and its observance but with the contents of I and II Enoch, II Baruch, and IV Ezra! A careful examination of any living religion (for example, Christianity) will find "how much else" is to be found in it besides its highest ethical and spiritual teaching. It is a question of emphasis: was this highest ethical and spiritual teaching recognised as such, or was it only the rare and occasional tradition of unique individuals? On such a view and by this test, the divergent orientation of the gospel and of first century Judaism as a whole will not long remain in doubt. But one wishes that Christians would stop talking about the "uniqueness" or the "superiority" of the gospel and begin demonstrating it in practice, and that Jews would not assume that when once a few parallels are found to the Sermon on the Mount they have discovered the inner principle or essence of Christianity.

Professor Moore's aim was to study Judaism at one stage of its development, the pre-Mishnaic, pre-Talmudic "age of the Tannaim". A long article in two numbers of the *Harvard Theological Review* (October 1924, January 1925) set forth his view of "the rise of normative Judaism", and this may be taken to have been the programme of his studies leading to the great work which he ultimately published. His approach was entirely that of the objective historian of religion. By some readers, his term "normative" has been understood to mean "normal"; by others, the word "rise" has been overlooked, with the result that they assume that Moore was describing the totality of Jewish religion in the first two centuries as a fixed and final thing—something which Judaism never became, certainly not until the fourth and fifth centuries, and not even then! The "normative" Judaism was the Judaism that emerged later, and maintained itself through the Middle Ages and beyond, and survives to this day. What we see in the age of the Tannaim was the "rise" of this more formal and more strictly defined faith and practice. It was an era of transition, influenced by the political and social conditions of the outer world and reacting against tendencies which were inimical to the very existence of this faith. The exaggerated "nationalism" and "exclusiveness" of ancient Judaism has sometimes been viewed as an example of peculiar perversity and "hatred of the human race"—as ancient critics called it. (They also accused Christians of the same thing.) But it is perfectly clear that exclusiveness was the price of survival in the age of religious syncretism which followed Alexander's conquest of the Near and Middle East, and of religious decline which at once followed the triumph of Roman arms throughout the Mediterranean world.

The crisis which syncretism brought upon the Jews is amply documented in I and II Maccabees and in other writings. For over two hundred years, under the Persians, the Jews had enjoyed complete religious freedom. For another century and more, under the relatively peaceful domination of the Ptolemies, the Jews in Palestine had been let alone, at least as far as religious cult and practice went, while those in Egypt seem to have enjoyed special favours and privileges. But with the beginning of the Seleucid regime in Palestine, in 198 B.C., conditions began to change. The political aims of Antiochus IV Epiphanes (175-163 B.C.) required the abandonment of Jewish peculiarities and the incorporation of Jewish religion, culture, and modes of daily life within the thought and culture of the empire: the southern flank of the Seleucid empire had to be consolidated and culturally unified with the rest. It is true that some modern historians, like Sir W. W. Tarn, take a more favourable view of the policy of Antiochus; but we are now viewing it from the Jewish angle—this is what it looked like to the Jews in Palestine. This programme of unification might have succeeded, if the Philhellene party at Jerusalem had prevailed. But opposition arose on the part of the "pious"—the *chasidim* (Greek, *hasidaioi*)—and the Graeco-Syrian *Kulturkrieg* was complicated by the internal struggle within Palestine itself which lasted for twenty-five years (168-143 B.C.). It ended with the freedom of the Jews to continue the practice of their ancestral religion, though the struggle left its permanent marks on their political and religious views. The later Maccabees might be worldlings, and Herod, still later (40-4 B.C.), a tyrant and adventurer; but there was no danger now that Judaism would be engulfed in the quicksands of syncretism and scepticism—where the cults of "lords many and gods many" were pooled in the tolerant assumption that no one knew much about the gods anyway, and that over all of human existence prevailed the will of a dark, inscrutable Destiny (Fate), while capricious Fortune (*Tychē*) made sport of individual lives.

Out of the strong movement of reaction against compromise with a totalitarian paganism, out of the reassertion of the religious independence of the nation, arose Pharisaism—originally the party of the Hasidim—one of the noblest religious movements in all history. This was quite in line with the principles of the restoration following the Exile, when the Second Commonwealth had been established by permission of Cyrus (520 B.C.), with the work of Nehemiah (444 B.C.) and the reforms of Ezra the scribe (397 B.C.). In the world in which early Judaism found itself, "exclusiveness"—as the pious discovered in the days of Antiochus—was the only condition under which it could survive. Our modern Western theories of toleration would have been simply unworkable in the ancient Near East. The Second Commonwealth had been founded upon a thoroughly religious basis: the centre of the nation's life was to be the temple with its continuous worship of Yahweh, and the sacred Law, the Torah, was to be the law of the land. The reorganised society in Palestine was to be the realisation, at long last, of the Covenant between God and his people —thus fulfilling the ancient promise, "All that the Lord has spoken we will do" (Exod. xix.8), in utter obedience to the divine mandates. The old Israel, before the Exile, had sinned and disobeyed, through generation after generation, and had been punished by Israel's God: this was the theory of priests and prophets alike, and it received formal expression

in a "deuteronomic" editing of the nation's history. But the
new society was to avoid the mistakes of the past and realise the
hopes of a blessed future upon earth, thus guaranteeing its
own indefinite survival, with prosperity in the present and a
prolonged posterity in the future, through strict observance of
the sacred code. Israel was to be "holy" as God was "holy"
(Exod. xix.6, Lev. xi.45).

This was the open and obvious reason—not bigotry and
fanaticism—for the stand which the Jews took in the days of
the Maccabean martyrs and through the generations that
followed. It also explains the firm views of the Pharisees and
their zealous practice of the theocratic faith. There were
prophets, it is true, and others who took a friendlier view of
the "nations round about", and pictured a time when "Israel
will be the third with Egypt and Assyria, a blessing in the
midst of the earth", and when Yahweh will say, "Blessed be
Egypt my people, and Assyria the work of my hands, and
Israel my heritage" (Isa. xix.24f.). The expulsion of the
Samaritans had not been without protest (Isa. lxiii.16), and
a later prophet had written the beautiful allegory of Jonah,
with its message of God's care for the heathen. But the main
concern of ancient Judaism as a religion was naturally and
necessarily its own self-preservation, since its existence was
constantly threatened by the struggles for power among the
surrounding nations, for whom religion was now, in the minds
of a majority of their leaders, chiefly a tool for the acquisition
or maintenance of political and economic domination. The
pictures drawn in those fascinating historical tracts, the books
of Daniel, Judith, and Esther, reflect the conditions of their
authors' own time, the second century before Christ, not those
of the old Assyrian or Babylonian eras, long before. Exclusiveness had its darker side, and its drawbacks, not least for the
nation or the religion which practised it; but for anyone to
criticise it from our easygoing twentieth century vantage point
is quite wrong, certainly for any Christian to do so. Had
Judaism gone down before the overwhelming threat of syncretism, the Christian religion—humanly speaking—would
never have come into existence, and the Dark Age that succeeded the fall of Rome in the fifth century might very well
have continued to this day.

3. *A System of Piety, Not of Theology*

It is a mistake to view ancient Judaism, especially during its rise in the Tannaite period and its development into what later became "normative" for the following centuries, as a system of belief or of doctrine; instead it was a system of piety. Pharisaism, its highest and best representative, was not a creed but a rule of life—somewhat like the "rules" of our Christian monastic orders with their lay affiliates, for example the Franciscan tertiaries. Those who wished to live strictly in accordance with the Law had once turned first of all to the teachers of Wisdom (see the Prologue to the "Wisdom of Jesus the Son of Sirach"—our book of Ecclesiasticus); these men were known as the "scribes" or writers, but they were not copyists only, they were teachers of the Law in which they were specially versed. The Pharisees were a lay society; they undertook, as laymen, to carry out the full requirements of Torah as it was expounded by these experts, the scribes. Of course their code or rule of life was "legalistic": how could it be anything else, since the Torah or "teaching", that is, the divine revelation, was mainly in the form of law? And how could a rule of life based upon the strict observance of the requirements of a religion escape being a set of rules? It will not do to criticise this from the point of view of modern anti-nomistic Protestantism. Our rejection of rules has gone much too far, so that today many Christians can scarcely be distinguished, by their outward observances, from their non-religious neighbours! But at least, it will be said, the Pharisees should have insisted upon preserving the spirit of devotion, of charity, of brotherhood, along with their rules. But this was precisely the ideal of Pharisaism, as stated by its best representatives, not as caricatured by its foes!

Why then did Jesus and the apostles reject Pharisaism? As a matter of fact, they did not reject it. What Jesus criticised and rejected was the very thing the best of the Pharisees criticised and rejected—extravagance in interpretation, cruelty and inhumanity in the name of religion, for example the casuistic interpretation of the "corban" rule, and rigorous prohibition of works of mercy on the Sabbath. He criticised hypocrisy and pretence, arrogant professionalism, and the whole tendency, seen in some of the worst representatives of scribism, to identify their code of rules with the "perfect will of God"—the tithing of "mint, dill, and cummin" to the neglect of "the weightier matters of the Law" (Matt. XXIII.23; cf. Luke XI.42). Jesus' criticism of scribal tradition and of Pharisaic practice did not keep the early Palestinian Christian community from observance of the Law and the temple cultus, or prevent Paul from claiming proudly to be "a Pharisee, a son of Pharisees" (Acts XXIII.6, XXIV.14, XXVI.5; cf. Phil. III.5), or the author of the book of Acts from representing Paul as on trial for his life because of his Pharisaism (Acts XXIII.6-10).

We may go even further and describe the theology of the New Testament, in its main outlines, as a Jewish theology in transition—a theology which was basically Pharisaic.[1] The transition took place when the Christian movement swept out into the broad intellectual and moral area of Graeco-Roman culture, took over the already well-organised moral and religious propaganda of the Jewish Diaspora, and began to express itself in new forms, new terms, and new patterns of thinking. It was at first simply a Jewish theology with a new emphasis—a far greater stress upon eschatology than ordinary Judaism gave it, though Judaism was certainly an eschatologically oriented religion, and with a Messiah who was not only coming but had already come. But the further development of New Testament religion represented a shift in loyalty, by which the person of Christ came to stand out ever more clearly in the foreground while devotion to the Law receded more and more into the background. Even apart from a consideration of the essential nature of Christianity, or the work of Paul, this shift must be viewed as an inevitable one, in view of the main types of religious devotion and thought which were steadily becoming more common in the Graeco-Roman world. Judaism was a system of piety, centred in devotion to God's Law—that is, in devotion to God through observance of that Law by which he had revealed himself to Israel; but Graeco-Roman religion was steadily becoming, in the later Hellenistic age, and especially as represented by many of its most ardent spirits, devotion to a divine Saviour and

---

[1] This is one of the underlying principles of my *Introduction to New Testament Thought* (New York, Abingdon-Cokesbury, 1950).

Preserver (*Sōtēr*), to a "God Manifest" not only in the past but in the present, a *Kyrios* or Lord who ruled the believer's whole course of life and was the invisible head of his community. Christianity certainly was not just one more of these cults of a divine *Kyrios* (whether of the "mystery" type or not); Christianity was different, not only because Jesus had been a historical person but because of the church's inheritance from Judaism. Its original and essential character as a type of Jewish belief marked it off from all other contemporary cults. It was because Christianity had arisen as a movement within Judaism, and had never lost its original, historical character, that this was so. It flatly refused to part with the Old Testament, or to abandon its own evangelic traditions, which were full of Jewish ideas and presuppositions, and were quite incomprehensible outside their Jewish setting—as Gnosticism was presently to prove.

As a system of piety rather than a system of doctrine, Judaism was characterised by a strong emphasis upon practice, with a minimal stress upon belief. In fact it was sometimes described—and has since been described—as a system of ethics and ceremonial with a slight framework of theological or doctrinal sanctions. Such a description is much exaggerated, of course; the truth is rather, as Père Bonsirven has said, that the "doctrines contained in Jewish theology are not expounded or even considered by themselves, as an end in themselves; they are all connected with living, and oriented toward practice. Life itself, a rule of life, this is what chiefly interested every Jewish soul. That is why, in their theodicy, the Jews scarcely thought of God in any other way than in his relations to his creatures; and in their studies and preoccupations they gave chief place to what is concerned with living—wisdom was the science of life, of physical life quite as much as spiritual. And it was also inevitable that, in their teaching, practical directions took precedence, in numbers and almost in importance, over pure theory. . . . It is in the domain of morals and religion that one sees most clearly the excellence of Judaism. On this point it surpasses the ancient religions and philosophies, as was to be expected of the nation which was the depository of revelation and the zealous guardian of ethical monotheism."[1]

[1] J. Bonsirven, S. J., *Le Judaïsme palestinien au temps de Jésus-Christ*, Vol. II (1935), p. 3.

4. Hellenistic Judaism in the Diaspora

A distinction must be drawn between the Judaism of Palestine, in the Tannaite period, and that of the Diaspora—for example, the school of Alexandria, with Philo as its chief representative, or, let us say, the type of Judaism presupposed by Paul, and perhaps current in the Jewish colony at Tarsus in his youth. But the distinction must not be exaggerated or made into a contrast—certainly not in the case of Philo, whose fundamental loyalty to the Palestinian tradition cannot be questioned, and who insisted that, for all his freedom in allegorical interpretation, this did not dispense anyone from observance of the letter of the Law. With Paul and some others, the case may have been different. Despite Luke's statement that Paul had studied at the feet of Gamaliel (Acts xxii.3), the Judaism which Paul knew seems to have been amalgamated with certain popular Hellenistic religious ideas: Sin, Death, the Law, for example, are not mere facts of experience or of history, but invisible, shadowy, quasi-personal forces which ruled mankind along with the other elemental spirits (*stoicheia*) of the universe. In a system of piety with no limits set to speculative thinking, such ideas were not held to be incompatible with religious loyalty; orthodoxy was, so to speak, a matter of practice, not of belief. There even existed, apparently, a Jewish type of Gnosticism in the first century—though the evidence is not overwhelming; and also some approximation to a Jewish "mystery"—though this may be only a matter of language, the terms being borrowed (for example by Philo,[1] for the purpose of elucidating his views), much as Paul used "mystery" terms now and then without making Christianity into a mystery religion.

Thus the early church, in its progress westward beyond the confines of Palestine, found the field already prepared for it. In the words of the most Hellenistic of the gospels, "Others have laboured, and you have entered into their labour" (John iv.38b). It was also true that "one sows and another reaps" (v. 37). For the early church not only shared the labour but took over the field, with the result that Judaism abandoned its

---

[1] See the exposition of Philo's thought in Professor E. R. Goodenough's *By Light, Light* (New Haven, Yale Univ. Press, 1935).

far-flung frontiers of missionary propaganda; it abandoned the Septuagint, the Greek translation of the Hebrew scriptures, which the Christians had adopted as their own and reinterpreted, for the far more literal versions of Aquila and Theodotion, and it insisted upon the use of Hebrew instead of Greek in the services of the synagogues of the Diaspora.

In view of the enormous use made by the early Gentile Christians of their Jewish heritage, the Septuagint and the works of Philo, the Jewish liturgy and the whole Graeco-Jewish religious vocabulary which the church took over,[1] it is strange that the Christian attitude toward Judaism was not more sympathetic. But dogmas are harder to get around than facts. And the anti-Jewish dogma was deeply fixed in Christian thought and devotion. "His blood be on us and on our children" (Matt. xxvii.25), "Your father the devil" (John viii.44), "The Wrath has come upon them to the uttermost"— or "at last" (i Thess. ii.16)—these dreadful utterances, which ought to find no place in any sacred book, stand out conspicuously in the New Testament. They are the flaming posters put up by the world-wide anti-Jewish propaganda of the early Christians and their pagan neighbours. This terrible inheritance of hatred and bigotry the early church passed on to the medieval, and the medieval to the Reformation and post-Reformation churches. Peter "the Venerable", the ninth abbot of Cluny (1092-1156), addressing the Jews on the futility of their religion, and avowing that he intended to benefit their souls—"if you *have* souls"—this is only one of the more despicable of Christian examples of medieval anti-Judaism. The whole ghastly story of fanatical hatred, tension, rioting, pillage, and murder which continued for centuries, especially in the Rhineland and the Low Countries, during the Crusades and after, is not often told in histories of the church, but the record is not complete without it. From this accumulation of prejudice and fanaticism the Reformation might have been expected to set European society free. But not so. The theological basis of the Reformation was Paulinism, chiefly as understood by Luther and Calvin, not the teaching of the gospels, which were demonstrably Jewish in tone and outlook as well as in language and presuppositions. The result was a

---

[1] See *The Bible and the Greeks*, by Professor C. H. Dodd (London, 1935).

C

total identification of Judaism with "self-righteousness", reliance for salvation on "works of the Law", and "confidence in the flesh". That Germany, the home of the Reformation, was a refuge for Jews during two centuries does not disprove the patent fact that basically the Protestant dogmas were anti-Jewish, nor that Luther's own personal influence was anti-Jewish. At long last, the rising tide of modern "anti-Semitism" got under way in Germany soon after the Franco-Prussian War of 1870, chiefly in army circles. The infinite tragedy which resulted, under Hitler, makes one wish that the years 1933-1945 could be blotted out of human history.

This is our situation today. We have inherited the bitter prejudices and the narrow, fanatical ideology cultivated through many centuries in both eastern and western Europe. So deeply ingrained is this prejudice that many of us, for whom religion means chiefly theology, doctrines, or even philosophical views, can scarcely think of Judaism as religion. And so far has this ideology gone that the Christian New Testament is interpreted from a purely dogmatic point of view: "the gospel" is not the teaching of Jesus, but the interpretation of Jesus, chiefly his death and resurrection, as set forth by Paul. Thus prejudice always rebounds upon those who share it. Our own sacred book is distorted, and our own religious life deformed, in the interest of maintaining a theological principle, namely, the "rejection" of the Jews and the divine condemnation of "moralism" and "legalism"! As we shall see, the consequences of this misinterpretation are far-reaching, not only for Jews but for Christians.

CHAPTER TWO

The Results of
Misinterpretation

The background of the New Testament is a double one, Graeco-Roman and Jewish. Hence the expert student and interpreter of the New Testament must be familiar with both—one alone is not enough. Without such a comprehension of the double background, unfortunate and partial judgments regarding the New Testament are almost inevitable, especially since the early church which produced the New Testament was in transition from one to the other, from Judaism to Hellenism, from the East to the West.

1. Examples of Misinterpretation

Examples of misconstruction and misapprehension of the Graeco-Roman background may be seen in the superficial views popular fifty years ago, for example in the "Christ Myth" theory; or the "mystery religion" hypothesis, which derived the church's sacraments from the Oriental mystery cults and its theology from a supposed "mystery theology". A single inscription, and that a very late one (end of the fourth century after Christ), was made to explain the whole practice of mystery initiation, at least in Mithraism, and hence in Christianity: the *mystēs* was *taurobolio in aeternum renatus* ("reborn unto eternity through the taurobolium", the bath in fresh bull's blood).[1] No one today would think of explaining even Mithraism, let alone Christianity, in this way: the

[1] See my *Hellenistic Religions* (New York, Liberal Arts Press, 1953), p. 147.

17

language of the inscription was probably borrowed from the Christians.

Examples of misconstruction of Judaism are today more plentiful than ever, thanks to the efforts to interpret the so-called Dead Sea Scrolls, discovered in 1947, and to show the dependence of the New Testament—especially the Gospel of John—upon the thought and language of these ancient writings. Not long ago a student came to me for help with a research "project" he had been assigned in a course in the Bible in another school. "Since the Dead Sea Scrolls emphasise the *unity* of the community, and since the Gospel of John makes Jesus say, 'I and the Father are one', is it not necessary to suppose that Jesus derived such language from the Qumrân community?" Only abysmal ignorance of both ancient Judaism and the New Testament can explain the assignment of such a "project".

Or take another example. One of the best known Christian preachers recently published a sermon for world-wide distribution. It had been preached on one of the most significant occasions in the public life of one of the leading countries of Europe. The thesis of the sermon was that between the years when he was twelve and thirty, Jesus (after confounding "the Professors in the temple") made a thorough study of Judaism, to see first of all if Judaism could be made to "live again"; then he studied the "ancient instinctive religion of the Hebrews prior to Moses, the magic primitive religion", and finally investigated the "loyal devotion to high altitudes of thought and action" which he found among the Essenes, among whom he lived for six or seven years. It was during these "hidden" years that he absorbed their spirit; and this is what accounts for "the singular correspondence between some of their wisest sayings and corporate acts and the sayings and acts of Jesus". Could anything be more fantastic and unreal than such a hypothesis? This is the kind of thing our superficial theological education, in this booming twentieth century, has made possible, and has subjected our churches to—as "captive audiences". It is on a level with the hypothesis that during his "hidden years" Jesus visited India, and there learned the "ancient wisdom of the East", which underlies (according to Theosophists) the whole gospel of Jesus and the Christian religion. It is no better than the hypothesis, advanced not long before World War II, that Jesus went to India, and there learned some of the truths of religion but, still unsatisfied, went on to Japan, where he tapped the deepest source of divine wisdom, returning to Palestine in A.D. 28 or 30 with his full and final revelation of divine truth.

What lies behind all this fantastic nonsense? Several things. One is the uncritical, unhistorical outlook of many religious persons, who have been trained to avoid, even to fear, historical and literary criticism of the Bible, and are consequently helpless before these seemingly plausible theories. Another is the type of reading common today, when novels are accepted in lieu of history and when fiction is preferred to the basic documents of the past. Still another is the inability of most persons to check what they read by reference to the original sources, which are often in another language; this is a very great even if unrecognised handicap of many clergymen, who undertake to expound or defend the scriptures without understanding the languages in which they are written. The impediment is a long-standing one, and goes even farther back than the Middle Ages, when the clergy knew only Latin; it was also to be found in Victorian times—as when the poet Tennyson remarked of Benjamin Jowett, on hearing that he did not read Hebrew, "Fancy the priests of a religion unable to read their own sacred books!" Unfortunately, it is still true of the majority of the clergy in some churches.

Still another factor making possible these preposterous explanations is the assumption which underlies much of modern theology, as it also did much of medieval, namely, the assumption that ancient Judaism was a moribund, formalistic, insincere religion, a dying faith by which men went through the motions of piety but had lost its spirit, a religion for which there was no longer any future of usefulness or vitality. The falsity of this view should be apparent at once: Judaism is still alive, and perhaps was never more alive than today, in spite of the repeated efforts of its enemies to exterminate it, chiefly in our own times. The question-begging term *Spät-judentum*, "Late Judaism", is an insult to a religion which is still "alive and on the march". The term came out of the theological controversies and polemics of the Reformation and

post-Reformation periods. It arose in the era of such scurrilous
works as Johann Andreas Eisenmenger's *Entdecktes Judenthum*
(1700), and it assumes that from the first century onward
Judaism was of no further account, even negatively, in religious
history, certainly not as related in any way to Christianity.

On the contrary, the debt of Christianity to Judaism is
incalculable—as is that of any child to his parents, not for
what he possesses but for what he is, in face and figure, in
blood and breeding, in character and mental equipment and
purpose in life. Both positively and negatively, first century
Judaism helped to shape the growing Christian religion and
to launch it upon the broad open sea of contemporary Graeco-
Roman civilisation. In later centuries, Christian scholars sat
at the feet of the rabbis, as did St. Jerome in preparing the
Vulgate (Latin) translation of the Bible. Later still, medieval
thinkers learned from Jewish philosophers, Christian exegetes
from Jewish—for example, from great scholars like Rashi and
Maimonides; and still later from critics like Spinoza, not to
mention grammarians, lexicographers, and editors of the Bible.
It is an impossible view that would segregate Judaism and
Christianity from each other, even though their contacts
through the centuries have often been accompanied by misunderstanding and conflict.

To return to the Qumrân scrolls for a moment, it is perfectly obvious to scholars familiar with the whole broad world
of first century religion that the contacts between the Dead
Sea Scrolls and the New Testament are few in number and
not really fundamental to either literature. Compared with
the hundreds of contacts and parallels between the New Testament and the religious and popular literature of the Hellenistic
age, both Jewish and Greek, the contacts with the Dead Sea
Scrolls are comparatively insignificant. One can find those
parallels cited in the commentaries, all the way from Wetstein's
great edition of the New Testament (Amsterdam, 2 vols.,
1751f.) to the modern *Handbuch zum Neuen Testament*, edited by
Hans Lietzmann, and the *Kommentar zum Neuen Testament aus
Talmud und Midrasch* by H. L. Strack and Paul Billerbeck. The
New Testament Lexicon of Walter Bauer, based on that of
Erwin Preuschen, now available in English (1957), and the
Theologisches Wörterbuch zum Neuen Testament, begun in 1933

by Gerhard Kittel, likewise contain citations of many parallels. If one takes the time to work patiently through such a commentary on John as Walter Bauer's or Rudolf Bultmann's, and checks the references for himself, and reads the relevant passages, especially the parallels, he will realise that the Qumrân contacts are merely "more of the same", a few more to be added to the hundreds of parallel words, phrases, ideas, found in the religious literature of the Hellenistic age. For Qumrân also belongs to the world of Graeco-Roman Hellenism! Judaism could not possibly escape contacts with this "outside" world, even in a monastic community at the northern end of the Dead Sea. "Hellenistic" influences permeated all sorts of religions and cults, whether they spoke, read, or wrote Greek or only their native tongues. Syncretism was the ambient atmosphere of the whole Near and Middle East from *circa* 300 B.C. down to the Mohammedan conquest. It was inescapable as wind and rain, sunshine and tempest, which sweep across whole continents, regardless of national and linguistic barriers. Hence the few and superficial resemblances between the New Testament and the Dead Sea Scrolls—which are far more than offset by the striking contrasts—do not prove the dependence of Christianity upon the Essenes, or even of John the Baptist upon them, but only the overwhelming dependence of both, or of all three, and of Judaism itself in a measure, upon the political, social, and religious conditions and the prevailing ethos of the whole Hellenistic age. No one escaped it, either the monks at Qumrân or the Pharisees in the country villages or John the Baptist in the wilderness or the followers of Jesus wherever they went in their bold preaching of the new faith. All belonged to the vast world of Hellenistic religious syncretism, even when reacting against it. Judaism had already begun a world-wide propaganda for the winning of proselytes, long before the Christian movement got under way, and the condition upon which this was undertaken involved both using the language, and therefore to some extent sharing the thought, of the whole Graeco-Roman world, at least everywhere west of the Euphrates.

The fact that both Judaism and Christianity made contributions to Hellenistic-Roman religious life, thought, and activity, often at unexpected levels (magic, for example, or the theosophical writings of the Hermetic groups, or the books of the Gnostics, or the fictitious Sibylline Oracles, or the conception of a political Messiah, or the literary criticism of "Longinus"), proves that these contacts were close, since the influence was both widespread and deep. Just how much Judaism contributed to the growing monotheism of the popular philosophical schools is difficult to say: but that it contributed something is unquestionable. Such modern scholars as C. H. Dodd (see his book *The Bible and the Greeks*, 1935), Walter Bauer (see his New Testament Lexicon), or Adolf Deissmann, whose classic *Light from the Ancient East* (1908, revised in 1922) is still as fascinating and rewarding as ever—these and other writers have made special studies of the religious vocabulary of late Hellenism. The results of their researches show not only that this vocabulary became an enormously influential factor in the formulation of Christian theology, but also that it had already been influenced by Judaism, along with the other religions of the Near and Middle East, by philosophical thought and discussion, and by age-old religious concepts deeply embedded in the Gentile mind. There are terms and ideas as old as Homer even in the earliest gospel, that of Mark!

Still another misconception may be cited: the description of Paul and even of Jesus as a "rabbi". Despite arguments to the contrary, the evidence indicates that the title was probably not in common use until after the refounding of the Jewish schools by Jochanan ben Zakkai soon after the fall of Jerusalem in A.D. 70. But more than that, the whole idea of the rabbinate was quite different from the one presupposed when the title is attributed to Jesus or to Paul. A popular religious teacher or *chasid* like Jesus was no rabbi; he was an independent expounder of the Bible and teacher of religion. Paul, despite the picture of him in Acts XXII.3 as a pupil of Gamaliel, shows very few traces of rabbinic influence or training. He was a layman from the provinces, a Hellenistic, that is, Greek-speaking, Jew of the Western Diaspora, and his "theology" contained mythical and allegorical elements which were unknown in orthodox Judaism, namely, in the Judaism which was becoming standard during the Tannaite period. Contrary to the popular modern view, the rabbis were not allegorists but lawyers, and insisted upon the primacy of the *literal* meaning of scripture.

Another now popular modern misconception is the universality of apocalyptic literature and thought, and even of messianism, and the centrality of the Messiah for the so-called messianic hope. For Christians, yes; since the Messiah was the central, crucial figure in all God's dealings with the world, and especially in the now-approaching full realisation of the ancient promises. But not for Jews; since the king-messiah— the anointed king—was only one figure in the drama of the coming End of the Age, and easily disappeared where conceptions of transcendent bliss or of a world-judgment on the Last Day took the place of the traditional nationalistic hopes of a restored Davidic monarchy. It is largely due to the centrality of Christology for much of Christian theology that the centrality of messiahship has been read back into ancient Judaism; but this is not the picture one gets from the ancient Jewish literature—see, for example, the summary in Paul Volz's *Eschatologie der jüdischen Gemeinde* (1934), one of the best accounts of ancient Jewish eschatology we possess.

Still other misconceptions could be listed: for example, the idea that Judaism was a purely legalistic cult, or purely ritualistic, a "book-keeping" religion by which men undertook to "establish their own righteousness" and win "merit" in the eyes of God. Some of Paul's language looks in this direction, but it cannot be taken at face value, nor viewed as applying to all Jews in the first century. (See the first two chapters of Luke for a fairer view, found within the New Testament itself.) Paul's language is that of the convert, who exaggerates the faults of the creed he has abandoned. Let us read instead the anecdotes of the early rabbis, or earlier still those of the great "pairs" among the Tannaim, as treasured in the Talmud and Midrash or collected in such a work as W. Bacher's *Die Agada der Tannaiten* (2 vols., 1890, Vol. 1 in 2nd ed., 1903). Or consult the oldest parts of the Jewish liturgy, the Shema with its three great prayers, or the Shemoneh Esreh, the Kaddish,[1] the Psalms, the priestly blessings. Here is where we should test the pulse and feel the warmth of any religion—in its prayers. The deepest questions about any religion are not to be put to its theologians, or its apologists and propagandists, or its zealous neophytes, or its schoolbook writers, but only to

---

[1] See Ch. III.

its saints. Or, to change the approach, ask the laymen, in any religion, to name their saints, and tell us what it is that makes them saints? Who is the pious man, anyway? The old Jewish answer would probably have been, "Our saints are those who live close to God and obey his will, who keep his Law and fulfill his purposes". This is what they said of the great teacher Hillel: "His piety is such that he brings men close under the wings of Shekinah", which means, he is one who makes men aware of the presence of God (see *Shabbath* 31a). Who could do more? And what is a saint if not one who does that? And how could he do it without living, in public and in private, in closest communion with his Father in heaven?

It is a great mistake to attempt to escape comparison by asserting that Christianity is "not *a* religion", that is, not one more of the many religions that have held the hearts of men over the centuries, but is rather a wholly new "way of life", of "access to the Father", which has been opened up by Christ; and should therefore be viewed as the final fulfilment of all the deepest yearnings and aspirations of the human race, faintly foreshadowed but never fully realised in the many faiths of mankind—a "religion" purely *sui generis*, supernatural, without any relation to history or to other creeds. To say all this sounds like praise, and it seems to lift Christianity above the range of criticism or of comparison with the other religions —including Judaism. But it is historically false, and it leads only to a misunderstanding of Christianity—by those who profess it, if not by others. This view of course denies that Christianity is either amenable to or interpretable by the principles which govern all religious development, psychology, and history. But it is no credit to the Christian religion to be described in this way. The words carry the same tone of unreality that accompanied the dictum popular in the nineteenth century, "Christ is man, not *a* man"! Christianity is, we believe, the true fulfilment of the age-old hopes of all mankind; but this is not proved by denying or ignoring the ways that have led from earlier religions to Christ. The same is true of Judaism, for Judaism and Christianity taken together represent the culmination of ethical monotheism, based upon divine revelation.

Still another factor in the situation which makes possible the many absurd historical judgments which have occupied us since the Dead Sea Scrolls were discovered is the dominance in contemporary theology of a school of thought which depreciates history and substitutes for it a revived dogmatism claiming to be "orthodoxy". The defects of this type of theology have often been pointed out, yet the school persists. Some of its advocates bid theological students not to waste their time in historical, philological, exegetical, or archeological studies. As far as one can see, this proposal amounts to nothing more nor less than that Protestantism should dig its own grave. If our religion ceases to encourage the study of history, or to promote historical research, or if it substitutes an antiquated dogmatic interpretation for the modern historical interpretation of the Bible, Protestantism will have ceased to exist. It matters not whence the dogmas are issued; if they discourage or forbid the free historical study of the Bible the day is over and done for the "open Bible" of the Protestant churches, the heirs of the Reformation.

2. *Permanent Value of the Church's Historical Background*

We have considered the dual heritage of Christianity, from the Graeco-Roman world and from Judaism. It may now be asked, How much of this twofold background remains a permanent part of the Christian religion? Was it a merely temporary structure, the scaffolding destined to come down when the building was finished, the form or mould intended to be broken up as soon as the cast became set? Or, on the contrary, did Judaism and the Greek religion make permanent contributions to Christian faith or practice? Despite the modern effort to discount the background—as in Ritschl's opposition to "Greek metaphysics" and in the anti-Judaism which still simmers under the surface of modern Protestantism —it remains true that historical Christianity has always recognised the abiding importance of both the Greek and the Jewish contributions. The early church fathers insisted that the preparation for the gospel—the *praeparatio evangelica*, as the Latins called it—was positive and real, not merely temporary and negative. So also did the older Protestant interpreters and historians of the Christian church, even as late as the end of the nineteenth century, who stressed the importance of Roman law, Greek philosophy, and Jewish religion in the "preparation of the way for Christ". This included not only Roman roads, but Roman justice; not only the Greek language, but Greek philosophy, Greek literature, Greek criticism of the mythology and ethics reflected in the religious traditions of all ancient peoples, including their own; not only Hebrew prophecy, viewed as the earliest announcement of the coming Messiah and his church, but Jewish religion, faith, zeal, loyalty, the martyr's fidelity to the God of his fathers and his absolute refusal to compromise with idolatry, bestiality, or atheism. In a word, all three factors, Roman, Greek, and Jewish, were powerful components in the widespread, indeed universal, Graeco-Roman culture which was steadily permeating the whole civilised world, from western India to the Atlantic Ocean, during the earliest period of church history.

Certainly some elements of this preparation were permanent —for example, monotheism. It was not only Judaism that stood for this principle; it was also found in increasing measure and emphasis in Greek philosophy and in popular religion. The movement did not sharply impinge upon early Christianity but went its own way, reaching its climax in the worship of *Sol Invictus*, the unconquerable sun, under the Severi in the third century. Nevertheless it had a relevance to the Christian revelation. But once more an indubitable, inalienable historical fact has been denied or minimised in recent times, and is being minimised even today. Certain phases of contemporary theological thought emphasise Christology apart from theism— as did the ancient Gnostics, who insisted that we cannot know the supreme God but only his messenger or interpreter, the Redeemer who has come to dispel our ignorance of the meaning of existence and to rouse us from spiritual slumber and bid us seek salvation through true knowledge (*Gnōsis*). A generation ago we were told that God was "Christ-like": Jesus we know, and Paul we know, but who is God?—This is mere "Jesuo-latry", of the kind which historic Christianity has always repudiated, namely, the worship of a man. In those days a famous theological scholar insisted that the early Christian conception of God was of *a* god, namely, Christ, the new

Christian deity, who had been imported from the East along with the other new deities of the time, a mystery god, destined to take the place of the old universal Father God of the Mediterranean peoples—Zeus "the Father of gods and men", Jupiter "Greatest and Best", *Optimus Maximus*. He was even destined to supplant Yahweh, the God of the Jews—as if this was conceivable! On the contrary, the emphasis in Christianity has always been theistic. The sovereignty of God, the primacy of God the Father, even his "priority"—with the consequent subordination of the Son and the Spirit—is the basic conception in Christian theology as in the whole Christian religion, its faith, rites, sacraments, worship, and law. Upon this doctrine depend such concepts as God's eternity, his creation of the world, the existence of angels and of human souls and their immortality—you cannot shift the centre and keep the system in order. Christianity is not a "Christolatrous" religion; it is *theistic*, from beginning to end.

Another important feature in both Judaism and Greek religious philosophy was the emphasis upon education in religion. Judaism stressed the study of the scriptures; Greek philosophy stressed the study of its classics and the pursuit of an educated, intelligent, rational belief. Both insisted, with the New Testament (1 Peter III.15), that one must be prepared to "give a reason" or "make a defence" of "the hope that is in you". The Jewish synagogue was "the house of study" as well as the place of prayer and praise. The very terms commonly used indicate this fact: for example, *Torah* (teaching), *darash, derush, darshan, midrash* (research), *halakah* (a rule of life set forth in scripture and tradition), *haggadah* (an example or illustration of the scriptural teaching). The Bible is still the great book of religion for both Judaism and Christianity. From the Christian point of view, the New Testament is really the supplement and completion of the Old, the climax of the inspired record of revelation and redemption. Hence the Bible —the whole Bible—must be studied carefully; as the Anglican Prayer Book insists, we are to "read, mark, learn, and inwardly digest" it.

Perhaps the most important feature in ancient Judaism was its recognition of the reality and its stress upon the importance of devotion and piety. This, it may be said, was only natural and necessary in a religion based upon law, that is, upon rules of observance, and it could easily slip into a formal routine lacking the spirit of devotion. But let the critic read the ancient Jewish literature. The piety therein reflected is not lacking in the spirit of devotion. Of course, it is a religion based upon a revelation of divine *requirements*: "He has showed you, O man, what is good; and what does the Lord require of you . . . ?" (Micah vi.8)—such a religion will inevitably insist upon the fulfilment of these demands, since they are made by God of his children. But read not only the Bible: read also the other religious literature, especially the liturgy with its ancient prayers. Their spirit is by no means that of a slavish observance of rules, but the highest conceptions of duty, with an exalted inner enthusiasm for goodness and a spirit of loving obedience to the will of God which had flown directly from the teaching of the great Old Testament prophets and psalmists. Many modern Christians, alas, are handicapped by an inherited distaste for piety; all our lives we have heard scorn and ridicule poured out upon "empty piety", "mere formalism", and "religious hypocrisy", until we scarcely recognise true devotion when we meet it. Anyone described as "pious" is at once suspected of being a fraud! But it was not always so, and it has not been so in Judaism. The "ancient pious men" were famous for their observance of religion—and also for their spirituality. Take Hillel, for example, in the saying already quoted: his gentleness, patience, and "loving-kindness" (for those about him), his "loyal love" (for God) "brought men close under the wings of Shekinah". In plain terms, his love for God and man made men aware of the divine presence. What more could one say of any saint? And who, in the last analysis, is the man who does most to convince other men of the reality of God, and of the firm foundations upon which rest both the life of devotion and the assurance of a life to come? Is it not the saint? *Not* the logician, not the systematic theologian, not the exegete or the historian, not the apologist, but the saint: the highest and noblest representative of any religion.

Read the maxims of that ancient piety—they are all from the Bible: "I keep the Lord always before me" (Ps. xvi.8);

"Turn my eyes from looking at vanities" (Ps. cxix.37); "The Lord is my portion; I promise to keep thy words" (*ib*., v. 57); "Thou shalt love the Lord thy God with all thy heart and soul and might" (Deut. vi.5; cf. Matt. xxii.37). All these, and many more, are axioms of Jewish faith; one and all they inculcate piety. The same is true of the New Testament: "Strive for holiness, without which no one will see the Lord" (Heb. xii.14); "Blessed are the pure in heart, for they shall see God" (Matt. v.8); "Love your enemies, and pray for those who persecute you" (*ib*., v. 44). In both ancient Judaism and early Christianity, the worship of God was central. Alas that for many of us today it has lost much of its importance! We are "activists", we say, and very "practical". We are prepared to undertake almost any task, if only we can get away from the pure, simple worship of God, which to many earnest people seems artificial, fulsome, and mechanical. We tend to think of religion chiefly as something that benefits us, something that must be exercised or "worked at". On such a view worship is only an aesthetic practice, indulged in by the few choice souls who enjoy it, and then only in the interest of their own self-improvement. Instead, worship is the pulsating heart of the religious life, and piety is its natural expression.

If we try to sum up what the modern world, especially the modern Christian world, may learn from Judaism, it is clear that these essential elements must all be considered: the indispensable centrality of belief in God, his uniqueness, his oneness, his sovereignty (not beclouded by metaphysical formulae); the possibility and the importance of religious education (rather than mere "evangelism"); and the final test of true piety. These elements are as essential to Christianity as they are to Judaism, though in the churches they were at one time more strongly emphasised than they are at present. The movements which ignore them are usually ephemeral, and do not express the vital, central life of religion; but our generation has experienced a spring tide of such movements—I mean those which depend chiefly upon philosophical views, or upon artistic or literary or even psychological or economic theories—not to mention emotional epidemics—rather than upon vital faith and godliness.

3. *Importance of the Study of Ancient Judaism*

In view of the permanent importance of ancient Judaism for early Christianity, it is obvious that a thorough knowledge of the mother-faith is absolutely indispensable for an understanding of the New Testament and the rise of the Christian religion.   Neither systematic theology, which of necessity belongs to a later period, nor philosophy of religion, a child of the eighteenth and nineteenth centuries, nor psychology of religion, the child of the twentieth, can take the place of a sympathetic, even enthusiastic, study of the parent religion of the Bible, ancient Judaism.   As a matter of fact, Christianity is not, and as a whole has never claimed to be, an independent, purely autonomous religion; instead, it is, and normally has always claimed to be, the end and climax of a long course of preparation, the final stage in a long series of divine acts of revelation and redemption which began with the first beginnings of the human race or even with the creation of the world.   The early Christian apologists used a phrase which was echoed by the eighteenth century deists, and which, in its true sense, was fundamentally sound: "Christianity as old as creation!"   Even as early as the second century the church was described as an ancient institution.   This meant, of course, that its history included both phases of the *praeparatio evangelica* described above: the age-old, historic, ever advancing divine revelation to Israel, and the long philosophic, religious, and moral tutelage of other nations, especially the Greeks.   These elements were not mere interesting forecasts or anticipations, they were indispensable, inalienable, organic parts of the whole historic process—formative, structural, creative.   They are still, for us, essential parts of the one divine movement which culminates in God's self-revelation and in man's discovery of God.

There are some persons who resent the expression, the Jewish "background" of Christianity, as if Judaism provided merely the contrasting foil to early Christian beliefs and practices.   Perhaps it would be better to say "the Jewish *origin* of Christianity" or the Jewish "antecedents".   But whatever descriptive term is used, the facts remain the same: both background and foreground are continuous, each a part of the other, as in any good landscape, and each requiring the

other for its full interpretation. The Old Testament background and antecedents of early Christianity have always
been recognised, except by those bizarre theorists who would
"get rid of the Old Testament". But the Jewish, that is, the
post-biblical Jewish, antecedents are an equally rich mine for
the interpreter, and invite the student to pursue and discover
its treasures for himself—not merely as illustrations of the
New Testament or of early patristic language or ideas or of
parallel religious thought and movements, but as positive
contributions to our own religious life here and now, in the
twentieth century. The ancient springs still flow, as in the
Psalms and the prophets, and are still cool and refreshing.
"Like as the hart desireth the water-brooks, so longeth my
soul after thee, O God"; "Thy word is a lantern unto my
feet, and a light unto my paths" (Ps. XLII.1, CXIX.105 BCP[1]).
The books that open up to us these treasures of interpretation
are readily available: such works as Israel Abrahams' *Studies
in Pharisaism and the Gospels*, Claude Montefiore's *Rabbinic
Anthology* (see p. 6 above), and S. Singer's edition and translation of the Jewish *Daily Prayer Book*, with Dr. Abrahams'
Companion to it. But the ancient literature itself contains
treasures still to be discovered and prized, words of wisdom
and of illumination for the living of the religious life, for the
dialogue of the soul with God, for the humble and obedient
"walk with God" which our forefathers knew and loved and
which gave them an inexhaustible reserve of inner strength
for the facing of hardship and frustration and bitter disillusion-
ment. This is something more than superficial "peace of
mind"; it is fresh light and a new source of power, an unceasing
wellspring of divine grace and "strength to help in time of
need".

4. *The Task of Interpretation*

The great appeal of the Reformation was to holy scripture,
taken in its plain, literal, historical sense, without appeal to
either the allegorical interpretation or the ecclesiastical

---

[1] The version in *The Book of Common Prayer*. The Prayer Book Psalter,
slightly revised, is still basically Miles Coverdale's translation (1535) from the
Latin Vulgate and the German. Though inaccurate in spot, it remains pre-
eminent in poetic beauty.

D

tradition which had hitherto accompanied and supplemented it.[1] Part of the Roman Catholic system of theology was treated as "mythological", as were also the legends of the saints, the historical fiction of the donation of Constantine, the theory of the two powers, secular and sacred, appointed by God to govern mankind, the treasury of merit, the theory of seven sacraments (instead of the two found in the gospels), the sacrifice of the mass, the doctrine of Purgatory and the practices which clustered about the belief, the sale of pardons and indulgences—all this "mythological" accretion to primitive Christianity was swept aside, and a purely "scriptural" system was substituted for it. But by the end of the nineteenth century, or certainly early in the twentieth, it began to appear that Protestantism likewise, though not equally, was "mythological". Devotion to the plain, literal sense of scripture had produced Fundamentalism on the one hand and Historicism on the other. It had been assumed, as a rule, that the whole body of Protestant doctrine must be found in the Bible; conversely, every text of scripture must find its place in the Protestant system. The third step—or stage—is upon us now, and the present-day Christian must decide whether to retain or reject the accumulated "mythology" of Protestantism as well as that of Catholicism. Perhaps very little can be done, or should be attempted. Perhaps Christianity, like all other religions, is inescapably "mythological", since it sets forth its doctrines in language and concepts which are essentially symbolic, antique, even primitive, and not wholly amenable to rationalisation. Perhaps the Christian rites and practices answer more deeply to human needs than to rational deductions from theological principles or to historical or legal enactments by Christ or the apostles, and have been provided under the guidance of the Holy Spirit during the centuries that have followed the apostolic age. Perhaps Christianity, like other religions, is more a creation of *art* than of science or philosophy, and must be understood as endeavouring to set forth in intelligible terms what is really beyond comprehension, even beyond adequate expression. Perhaps Christian art, architecture, painting, sculpture, music, liturgy, hymnody, drama, poetry,

[1] See my article "Exegesis" in Vol. x of the new edition of the *Encyclopedia Americana* (New York, 1952 and later).

ethics, even Christian theology itself, is not so much a homo-
geneous, consistent intellectual creation as a vast efflorescence
of the human spirit in response to the divine Spirit. Its forms
were derived chiefly from the surrounding culture of the
Hellenistic-Roman age, followed by the medieval age; and it
need not—indeed cannot—be forced into the narrow channels
of either literalism or historicism, that is, either literal ideas or
literal history, chronologically exact and annalistic. Some
things, as the Neoplatonist theologian Sallustius observed,[1] have
never come into being yet always are; and among these are
the deepest truths and realities of religion. What is wanted,
therefore, is something more than the now popular proposal
of "demythologisation", followed by a "remythologisation",
perhaps in the terms of modern science or of "existentialist"
philosophy; what is really required is nothing less than what
Paul Tillich has called "deliteralisation", that is, a poetic
interpretation, adequate to the poetic, artistic affirmation of the
profoundest religious insights and experiences. These affirmations have been recorded in language which is thoroughly
non-literalistic, in stories, parables, and figures which are
only symbols and projections of the deepest thought and feeling
—literal description is impossible, at this level. The unique
book which combines the fascinating story of man's quest for
God with the even more enthralling tale of God's search for
man—it opens with the call, "O Adam, where are you?"—is
anything but a "plain tale" to be interpreted in dull, prosaic,
literal terms.

In every generation, it seems, we must relearn the lesson of
criticism, namely, that it is wrong, both dangerous and misleading, to lay aside the methods of literary and historical
research and approach the biblical text directly from the side
of dogmatic theology. It is equally a mistake to decide
questions of exegesis by appeal to ecclesiastical pronouncements
or to private and purely personal religious predilections.
(There is surely a proper place for ecclesiastical decisions,
pronouncements, and definitions; but they must not be invoked in determining the exegesis of the New Testament or

---

[1] See A. D. Nock, *Sallustius: Concerning the Gods and the Universe*, §§ 2, 7, etc.
(Cambridge, 1926). The tractate is reprinted at the end of my *Hellenistic Religions*
(New York, Liberal Arts Press, 1953).

the historical probabilities that lie behind it.) Both these methods, ecclesiastical decision and private preference, were repudiated at the Reformation, but they are still in use, sometimes in unexpected quarters. For example, the exegesis of II Cor. v.19, "God was in Christ, reconciling the world to himself", is widely accepted in Protestant circles as a statement of the doctrine of the Incarnation as well as of the doctrine of the Atonement. But the comma after "Christ" is pure invention, and makes impossible a true understanding of Paul's suspended participle (a favourite stylism of Paul, as also of Luke: see p. 166). It imputes to Paul a hitherto unheard-of conception of the nature of Christ; and it implies an entirely unorthodox theological dogma (fourth century Apollinarianism) which the church eventually repudiated. Paul's language is the reverse: "Christ was in God" (for example, Col. III.3). The "God in Christ" formula is Johannine, not Pauline—John XIV.10 may indeed have suggested the Apollinarian Christology. Clearly, the correct translation is, "In Christ, God was reconciling the world to himself" (cf. RSV mg.). A better knowledge of Paul's religious background in Judaism, and consequently of his outlook as a Christian, would have made impossible this popular modern misinterpretation.

Take another example: the substitution of Jesus' "messianic consciousness" for the traditional threefold office of Christ as "prophet, priest, and king", set forth in the older biblical theology—obviously in a symbolic sense. The older terminology was derived from the biblical documents; the new is derived from modern psychology, and is obscure, debatable, and at best far from adequate. To describe Jesus of Nazareth as the head of a messianic movement that failed, a revolution that never came off, a "king", in Robert Eisler's phrase, "who never reigned", is more suggestive of the Mahdi than of the Incarnate Son of God. After all, the attempt to avoid Greek terms and Greek meanings and values in interpreting the New Testament has not produced anything of great merit. The pure Hebraism and Judaism of the earliest Christian community, with its type of thinking largely conditioned and influenced by the Old Testament, is of course an indispensable presupposition; but this is not identical with apocalyptic eschatology as found in I Enoch or IV Ezra or the Dead Sea

Scrolls—far from it! These last-named works are already deeply immersed in syncretism (not Hellenistic but Oriental), and however valuable for our understanding of the early development of doctrine (as Ethelbert Stauffer insists) the apocalyptic writings do not help us very much toward the understanding of either Jesus himself or the earliest Greek expression of Christian beliefs and hopes, in the gospel sources. Jesus' religion was the Judaism of the Old Testament, of the scribes and the Pharisees, not that of the apocalyptists or of the Qumrân sect. Once more, a sounder knowledge of ancient Judaism would save Christian teachers and students from a false appraisal of apocalyptic, as if it held the centre of the stage in the first century.

Still another example is the common misinterpretation of Paul's doctrine of the resurrection (as in 1 Cor. xv), understood as involving the restoration of the *body*, that is, the flesh—as in the Old Roman Creed, with its phrase *resurrectio carnis*. It also survives in the *Thirty-nine Articles* (Art. iv), "Christ did truly rise again from death, and took again his body, with flesh, bones, and all things appertaining to the perfection of Man's nature; wherewith he ascended into Heaven, and there sitteth, until he return to judge all Men at the last day." But, obviously, literary criticism has again been neglected; for the same apostle refers, in the same epistle, to survival of the spirit (v.5) as the survival of the man himself (iii.15). It is impossible to force our modern Western consistency of terminology upon such a non-theological thinker as Paul. The crude identification of a man with his flesh, that is, his body, is age-old. It meets us at the very beginning of European literature, in the opening lines of Homer. The heroes at Troy perished on the battlefield; their souls were thrust down to Hades; "they themselves" (*autous de*) still lay on the bloody ground, food for wild dogs and birds. You may say that the distinction—or the identification—is inevitable in human thought; but this does not justify a false exegesis of the language of Paul. The same range and variety in terminology and in thought is to be found in the ancient Jewish literature, from Daniel to Akiba and the second century Midrash.

Surely these examples suffice to show the serious consequences of the misinterpretation of the New Testament, a
misinterpretation which is practically inevitable if one neglects
or ignores its proper historical background and milieu, and
trusts either to his own inner consciousness or to ecclesiastical
tradition, viewed in isolation from its own historical background
and milieu, or takes dogmatic theology as his sufficient guide.
The extent to which anti-Jewish prejudice has misled interpreters of the New Testament, both ancient and modern, is
clear from the examples given above. Surely the better way
is to study the New Testament in the light of contemporary
ancient Judaism and Hellenism, taking both at their highest
and most positive, most creative best, and not as merely
negative foils against which to contrast the excellence of the
gospel. The answers to the questions raised in this chapter,
and to others like them, must be found by patient research,
not by appeal to dogmatic authority or to ancient church
"tradition", which as a rule reeks with prejudice and bigotry
wherever Judaism is concerned.

In the following chapters we shall examine the results of
research and their bearing on various aspects of the problem
before us; namely, the modern study of the ancient Jewish
synagogue with its liturgy; its origin, nature, and function as
a social and religious institution; the religious teachings of
ancient Judaism, as far as these can be summed up in a series
of quasi-theological principles or categories; the phenomenon
of apocalyptic eschatology, its relation to Judaism as a whole,
and its relevance to the early church; the relation of apocalyptic to prophecy, and the clear distinction between the two.
These chapters will deal with some of the most crucial questions
relating to ancient Judaism as it is reflected in the New Testament, and with the attitudes of Jews to Christians and of
Christians to Jews during the critical first two centuries.

Part Two

ANCIENT JUDAISM

CHAPTER THREE

The Ancient Synagogue

The ancient synagogue was simply the assembly or meeting (in Greek, the *sunagōgē*) of the Jewish community for religious purposes—purposes not limited to worship. The term came naturally to mean also the place of meeting, a building in which the community assembled for religious and other purposes. In Late Hebrew and Aramaic two terms were used for the two ideas: *kenēseth* and *bēth hakenēseth*, i.e. the "assembly" or "congregation" and the "house of the assembly". Thus the synagogue was primarily a place for prayer and the study of scripture, though characteristically the Greek word for the former, *proseuchē*, "place of prayer" (cf. Acts XVI.13, 16), is better known than the Hebrew, while the Hebrew word for the latter, *bēth hammidrash*, "house of study", is better known than the Greek. The synagogue was essentially a layman's institute for the reading and study of scripture, though the help of the learned was welcome (see Neh. VIII.4-8); Philo describes it as the "house of study" (*Life of Moses*, II. 216; *Special Laws: On the Sabbath*, II. 62, *didaskaleion phronēseōs*); so does Josephus (*Against Apion*, II. 175); and see Acts XV.21.

1. *Origin of the Synagogue*

The institution originated probably some time after or possibly just before the destruction of the First Temple in 586 B.C., perhaps in the Eastern Diaspora, that is, in Babylonia, but more probably in Palestine, where the synagogue in a measure took the place of the ruined temple. It had been a custom in Israel, long before the Exile, for the people to visit the priest and the prophet on Sabbaths and New Moons and receive

39

religious instruction from them (II Kings IV.23, Ezek. VIII.1, XX.1-3). Evidence for pre-Maccabean synagogues in Palestine has been found by some scholars in Psalm LXXIV.8, "the meeting places of God in the land". According to the Mishnah (*Tamid* V.1, VII.1) there were synagogues even inside the later temple. But this must mean that assemblies or religious meetings were held in the temple courts, not that synagogue buildings were erected there. After A.D. 70, when the Second Temple was destroyed by the Romans, the synagogue once more took the place of this central sacred edifice of Jewish worship with its sacrificial system, and prayer came to be viewed as the chief offering of service to God. It is said that "the Men of the Great Synagogue", that is, presumably, Ezra and his associates and successors, were the organisers of the synagogue (*Berachoth* 33a, *Pirqe Aboth* 1.1). This is no doubt in general correct, as to time and place, though the details are hazy and impossible to check. Certainly in the earliest parts of the liturgy, as in the contemporary literature, there are references and emphases which are best explained as coming from this traditional source and period—references to eschatology, angelology, the recitation of prayers at sunrise, and other features that reflect the surrounding Mazdaism of the Persian regime; and also emphases upon the unity of God, his sovereignty, his sole power as Creator and Sovereign, which reflect the determination of Judaism to repudiate and counteract Mazdean dualism (cf. Isa. XLV.7).

Though the place of the priest was never questioned, even after the fall of the temple, and his position as the teacher of religion, that is, the "teacher of righteousness", was everywhere acknowledged, the actual organisation of the synagogue was completely congregational. Wherever ten adult male Jews resided and agreed to attend the services or meetings for study, there a synagogue could be formed; usually they had to be men of sufficient leisure to enable them to attend daily worship and Bible reading. The synagogue was really an institute for advanced religious study. It was not a school for children, who had their own building or meeting place, but the assembly (or the assembly place) for adult study of the Torah, the Law of God in all its fullness as containing both the divine self-revelation and also the corresponding divine demand upon human loyalty and obedience. The synagogue, in brief, was the adult male community assembled to pray and to study the word—i.e. the words—of God: its officers were the officers of the community, now functioning at public worship. There was no separate organisation of elders, rulers, clerks, trustees, ministers, and so on, as in a Christian church, or as in a modern Jewish synagogue, and the priest living nearby was not *ipso facto* head of the congregation or "rector of the parish". His expert knowledge was frequently called upon; but he was not expected to preside. The "ruler of the synagogue" was the leading layman, something like a "ruling elder" or "senior warden", not a clergyman; today he is called "president of the congregation". Any visiting scholar, especially if he was known to be an accomplished student of scripture, might be asked to share in the service, to expound the passage or passages read, and deliver a homily. But he did not have to be an ordained rabbi—not even after ordination became the usual practice, sometime late in the first century. Obviously the scribes were often thus called upon: they too were laymen, devoted first to accurate professional copying of the Bible, then to its correct interpretation. Such a passage as the classic *Praise of the Scribe*, in Sirach xxxix, is a vivid idealisation of such a person.

Another group was the "ancient pious men", the Hasidim, who were primarily men of devotion, of prayer, and who made the synagogue a true meeting place with God. We Christians can understand this, for there are some churches which immediately put us in the mood of prayer: for generations, perhaps for centuries, devout men and women have poured out their hearts to God in this place, and we feel his very presence here. In such a place it is easy to pray. These Hasidim were a well-known religious group even before the Maccabean uprising in 168 B.C., for the question at once arose whether or not they would support Mattathias and his sons. They did support them for a time, but withdrew when they became convinced that the Maccabees planned a worldly kingdom and not the pure ideal theocracy which the Second Commonwealth had been designed to realise. Historically, the Hasidim were the forerunners, if not the founders, of the later Pharisees, the pious "Separatists" in the time of Jesus. It is also thought that the pious poor whose cries reverberate through the later Psalms were probably identical with this post-exilic yet pre-Maccabean group. They were the ones for whom, to use the phrase of Martin Dibelius, the "poverty-piety equation" was axiomatic: to be godly meant to be poor (see Psalm LXXIII), since they renounced the hidden deeds of darkness and the unscrupulous, dishonest methods by which the godless had amassed their fortunes. Conversely, to be poor meant to be godly—or at least it was a fairly clear indication of one's inner piety. Therefore, blessed be poverty! (Cf. Luke VI.20). But these men were also pietists, first of all, and devout worshippers of God, like Daniel (see Dan. VI.11) or the pious widow Judith (see Judith VIII.4-6). In fact, they were Hasidim.

2. *The Synagogue Liturgy*

The morning liturgy in the temple is described in the Mishnah (*Tamid* V.1 and VII.2). First came a call to worship (cf. Neh. IX.5), followed by the recitation of the Decalogue, then the three sections of the daily Shema (Deut. VI.4-9, XI. 13-21; Num. XV.37-41) and the three accompanying benedictions or prayers (see pp. 49ff.). After this—at least in later times—there was an affirmation of faith, a petition for the acceptance of the worship now being offered, and a prayer for peace. The benediction by the high priest and his associates concluded the service (Num. VI.23-27; cf. Sir. L.20f.), which was followed, like a "Last Gospel", by the psalm for the day sung by the Levites. This liturgical service in the temple accompanied or supplemented the sacrificial ritual which is prescribed in great detail in the Pentateuch and also in the division on sacrifices (*Kodashim*, that is, holy things, offerings) in the Mishnah and Talmud. Although all Israel (Num. XXVIII.2) was supposed to be present at the morning and evening sacrifice, it was obvious that this was impossible, after the nation had expanded—or been exiled—beyond the borders of Jerusalem and its immediate neighbourhood. The solution was simple: twice a year lay delegations went up to Jerusalem, with their priests, from the twenty-four districts into which the country was divided (1 Chron. XXIII-XXV), and for one week they "stood by" while the sacrifices were being offered. At home, the rest of the people assembled in the synagogues and read verses from the first chapter of Genesis relating to the particular day of the week, and offered prayers for various needs (see *Taanith* IV.2-3, *Megillath Taanith* I). The deep piety of the widow Judith was marked by her devotions on the flat roof of her house each day at the "hours of prayer", that is, when the prayers were being offered in the temple at Jerusalem. It was like an Anglican making his "spiritual communion" at the hour of the church service, if prevented from attending by illness or other serious cause.

Thus it was out of a profound religious devotion that the institution of the synagogue arose, possibly, as many Jewish scholars hold, even before the destruction of the Temple of Solomon in 586 B.C. During the Exile, this strong spirit of devotion survived, and the craving for communion with God led to the observance of as much of the old service as was practicable under the new conditions—loss of the temple, distance from Jerusalem, strange conditions in an alien land, or strange conditions even in their own land now under alien masters. Under these new conditions, prayer took the place of sacrifice—prayer and study of the written word of divine revelation. Judaism thus became the "religion of the book" which it has remained ever since, passing on the legacy to its two daughter religions, Christianity and Islam. Prayer, that is, the Shema, was now said three times each day, not just twice (cf. Ps. LV.17). (Compare the Christian rule in the second century *Didache*, VIII.3.) The hours were morning (dawn), early afternoon, and evening, corresponding to the hours of the old morning and evening sacrifices and the final burning of the scraps and other remains on the altar at the end of the day. On festivals there was an "additional" service (that is, a Musaf) which is still provided in the Jewish Prayer Book. This corresponds to the additional offerings prescribed in Numbers XXVIII-XXIX. On the Day of Atonement, once a year, there was even a fifth service, corresponding, it is said, to the old custom of closing the temple gates at evening.

By the end of the first Christian century, a fixed liturgy of prayer was authorised to take the place of the old temple service. It now began with the Shema and its three benedictions, followed by the Shemoneh Esreh ("Eighteen"), that is, the Eighteen Benedictions, which were blessings or prayers based originally on the Psalms and the prophets and introduced by Psalm LI.15 (see pp. 46ff.). On Sabbaths and festivals its central section was replaced by a briefer prayer for the day (somewhat as Christian liturgies provide a "collect for the day"); this reduced the number of benedictions in the Shemoneh Esreh from eighteen to seven. There are several different recensions of the Shemoneh Esreh, as it was recited in different countries, Palestine, Babylonia, Yemen, Egypt, and elsewhere. Another name for this long prayer was the *Amidah* (from *amadh*, stand), since, like most ancient prayers, especially in public, it was said standing. Then followed the two scripture lessons. (The word "lesson" in English, like *la leçon* in French, comes from the Latin *lectio*, the "selection" for "reading" in public, that is, at worship.) These two lessons were taken from the Law and the Prophets. The first and more important was the one from the Law, or *Torah*, which later was divided into 154 sections for Sabbath pericopes (*parashas*), thus providing enough passages for a three- or a three-and-a-half-year cycle. This was one-half of a sabbatical period of seven years, and consequently fitted into the liturgical scheme with great precision. The second lesson, from the Prophets, called the *haftarah*, followed—but only at the Sabbath morning service. Such a lesson as the one read by Jesus at Nazareth (Luke IV.16ff.) may have been the prescribed lesson for the day; if so, the service at which he read it must have been the Sabbath morning one. But it is more probable that the calendar of lessons had not yet been established, and that Jesus freely chose the passage from Isaiah LXI. The books of the Hagiographa were not read at the synagogue service in the first century—though various psalms were in use as "psalms for the day". These two scripture lessons were at once translated into Aramaic, the everyday language of first-century Palestine; the translator was called the *methurgeman* (from which our word "dragoman" is derived). Outside Palestine, the usual language of the translation must have been Greek, which was understood throughout the Mediterranean world and the Near and Middle East, at least as far as Babylonia, though in Mesopotamia the Jews still read and presumably also spoke Aramaic —see the introduction to Josephus' *Jewish War* and also the later Babylonian Talmud. The lessons from the Pentateuch were translated one verse at a time, to avoid making any mistake, omission, or addition; those from the Prophets were translated three verses at a time—which shows that the verse divisions of the Old Testament were very old, though it cannot be proved that they existed in the first century. Both the reader and the methurgeman stood at the reading desk in front of the assembled congregation. There are quaint stories of their rivalry, each claiming to be the more important—like the clerical anecdotes popular in all countries and ages. Then followed a sermon, at least on important days. The preacher— who was really a teacher—sat (Luke IV.20, Matt. v.1), and any likely visitor might be asked to give the sermon, homily, or exhortation (Luke IV.17, Acts XIII.15) Finally the traditional priestly blessing was pronounced. (See Num. VI.24ff.) This was said by a layman if no priest was present, but in the form, "May he bless". (Anglicans observe a similar nuance in various liturgical formulas.) At the end, alms were sometimes collected as an offering. Additional prayers and exhortations were sometimes added, informally.

3. *The Shemoneh Esreh*

The continuity of both the religious vocabulary and the religious ideas of first century Judaism with the noblest language and the purest concepts to be found in the Old Testament becomes obvious when we examine the synagogue liturgy. A vital religion does not live by its creed, or its theology, or its code of ethics, but by its worship; stated another way, its theology and its ethics are dependent upon and are nurtured by its worship. Here is where the religious pulse beats most firmly and can be felt most strongly: *lex orandi lex credendi est.* Fortunately, as we have seen, we can now reconstruct the first century Palestinian synagogue liturgy with a fair degree of certainty, thanks to the labours of many modern scholars, beginning with Leopold Zunz and ending with Israel Lévi, Ismar Elbogen, Louis Finkelstein, A. Marmorstein, Jacob Mann, and others; and thanks also, and especially, to the discovery and publication by Solomon Schechter of early liturgical fragments in the Cairo Geniza, which made it possible to reconstruct with more confidence the actual form of the

Shemoneh Esreh as it was used in Palestine in the first century—
the very heart or "canon", as we have seen, of the synagogue
service. This prayer, now greatly amplified, is still in use, and
still bears the name "Shemoneh Esreh" (that is, "Eighteen"),
though since the end of the first century it has actually contained nineteen rather than eighteen benedictions. In the
form in which it was probably in common use in Palestine
either in the days of Jesus or soon after, it read as follows. The
translation is in what Anglicans call "Prayer Book English",
since every phrase echoes the language of the Old Testament,
bears the archaic flavour of a liturgy long in use, and is steeped
in the devotional feeling of the ancient Hebrew Psalter. Later
additions are in square brackets.

THE EIGHTEEN BENEDICTIONS

Shemoneh Esreh

(An ancient Palestinian recension)

O Lord, open thou my lips,
And my mouth shall show forth thy praise.

1. Blessed art thou, O Lord,
   The Most High God, Maker of heaven and earth,
   Our Shield and the Shield of our fathers.
   Blessed art thou, O Lord, the Shield of Abraham!

2. Thou art mighty for ever,
   Thou sustainest the living
   And givest life to the dead.
   Blessed art thou, O Lord, who makest the dead to live!

3. Holy art thou and terrible is thy Name,
   And there is no God beside thee.
   Blessed art thou, O Lord, the holy God!

4. Bless us, our Father, with the knowledge that cometh from
   thee,
   And with intelligence and understanding from thy Law.
   Blessed art thou, O Lord, gracious giver of knowledge!

5. Turn us to thyself again, O Lord, and so shall we return;
   Renew our days as in the days of old.
   Blessed art thou, O Lord, who hast pleasure in repentance!

6. Forgive us, our Father, for we have sinned against thee;
   Wash away our transgressions from before thine eyes.
   Blessed art thou, O Lord, who dost abundantly forgive!

7. Look upon our distress, and wage our battle,
   And deliver us for thy Name's sake.
   Blessed art thou, O Lord, the Redeemer of Israel!

8. Heal, O Lord our God, the sorrows of our hearts,
   And send forth healing for our wounds.
   Blessed art thou, O Lord, who healest the sick among thy people Israel!

9. Bless to us, O Lord our God, this year,
   And fill the world with the treasures of thy goodness.
   Blessed art thou, O Lord, who blessest the year!

10. Blow the great trumpet for our deliverance,
    And raise up the banner for the gathering of our dispersed.
    Blessed art thou, O Lord, who gatherest the dispersed of thy people Israel!

11. Restore our judges as in former days,
    And our counsellors as at the beginning,
    And be thou alone Ruler over us.
    Blessed art thou, O Lord, who lovest judgment!

[12. As for the apostates, let there be no hope,
    And in judgment cause the kingdom of arrogance soon to be destroyed.
    Blessed art thou, O Lord, who humblest the proud!]

13. Upon the proselytes of righteousness bestow thy mercies,
    And grant us a good reward with those who do thy will.
    Blessed art thou, O Lord, the confidence of the righteous!

14. Have mercy, O Lord our God, upon thy city Jerusalem,
    And upon Zion, where thy glory dwelleth,
    And upon the kingdom of the house of David thine Anointed.
    Blessed art thou, O Lord, the God of David [who buildest Jerusalem]!

E

15. Hearken, O Lord our God, to the voice of our petition,
For thou art a gracious and merciful God.
Blessed art thou, O Lord, who hearest prayer!

16. Be gracious, O Lord our God, and dwell in Zion,
And let thy servants serve thee in Jerusalem.
Blessed art thou, O Lord; for thee will we worship in fear!

17. We give thee thanks, O Lord our God,
For all the blessings of thy goodness.
Blessed art thou, O Lord, to whom it is a good thing to give thanks!

18. Send forth thy peace upon Israel, thy people,
And bless us all as one.
Blessed art thou, O Lord, who makest peace!

As arranged chronologically by modern scholars, partly on the basis of the language used (especially the invocations) and partly on that of the parallels to contemporary ancient literature and tradition, the order in which the Shemoneh Esreh developed was probably as follows:

I. Pre-Maccabean: 1. *Fathers*, 15. *The Hearing of Prayer.*
II. Maccabean (168-165 B.C.): 14. *Jerusalem.*
III. Pre-Christian, perhaps pre-Maccabean: 16. *Worship*, 17. *Thanksgiving.*
IV. Between 149 and 30 B.C.: 9. *The Blessing of the Year.*
V. First Century B.C.: 2. *Powers*, 8. *Healing.*
VI. Between 20 B.C. and A.D. 10: 6. *Forgiveness.*
VII. Between A.D. 10 and 40: 3. *Sanctification of the Name*, 4. *Understanding*, 5. *Repentance.*
VIII. Between A.D. 40 and 70: 7. *Redemption*, 10. *Gathering of the Dispersed*, 11. *Restoration of the Judges*, 18. *The Blessing of Peace.*
IX. Between A.D. 70 and 117: 12, *Against the Apostates* (or *Against Heresy*), 13. *The Blessing upon Proselytes.*

AN EARLY FORM OF KADDISH

Similar in thought and feeling, and undoubtedly equally ancient is the old Aramaic *Kaddish*, which appears in the Prayer Book in five slightly different forms. The prayer was used at the end of a service, a homily, or a lecture, and was in effect a concluding benediction, like the ascription at the end of a Jewish or Christian sermon today. Its similarity to the Lord's Prayer is quite obvious—or rather, let us say, the likeness of the one to the other, for there is no evidence of dependence either way. Both prayers grew out of the deep religious devotion of the ancient synagogue.

May his great Name be magnified and hallowed in the world which he has created according to his pleasure [or his will].

May he set up his Reign [and cause his Redemption to spring forth, and bring near his Anointed, and ransom his people] in your days and during your years, and during the years of the whole house of Israel, and in a time near at hand. [And let them say, Amen.]

May his great Name be blessed for ever, unto the ages of ages!

The Shema with its Accompanying Prayers

Equally ancient, it seems, are the brief original forms of the three prayers which framed the daily Shema:

I. *Yoser.*—Blessed art thou, O Lord our God, King of the universe, who formest light and createst darkness, who makest peace and createst all things; who in mercy givest light to the world and to them that dwell therein; who in thy goodness renewest the work of creation every day continually, and who hast arranged the lights in heaven, rejoicing the world which thou hast created: *Blessed art thou, O Lord, Creator of the luminaries!*

II. *Ahabah.*—With abounding love hast thou loved us, O Lord our God; with great and exceeding pity hast thou pitied us, our Father, our King; it is us whom thou hast chosen out of all peoples and tongues; in love hast thou brought us near to thy great Name, our King, that we may praise thee and proclaim thy unity: *Blessed art thou, who hast chosen thy people Israel in love!*

[The Shema]

Hear, O Israel: The Lord our God, the Lord is One! And thou shalt love the Lord thy God with all thy heart and with all thy soul and with all thy might. And these words, which I command thee this day, shall be upon thy heart; and thou shalt teach them diligently unto thy children, and shalt talk of them when thou sittest in thy house, and when thou walkest by the way, and when thou liest down, and when thou risest up. And thou shalt bind them for a sign upon thy hand, and they shall be for frontlets between thine eyes. And thou shalt write them upon the doorposts of thy house, and upon thy gates. (Deut. VI.4-9.)

And it shall come to pass, if ye shall hearken diligently unto my commandments which I command you this day, to love the Lord your God, and to serve him with all your heart and with all your soul, that I will give the rain of your land in its season, the former rain and the latter rain, that thou mayest gather in thy grain, and thy new wine, and thine oil. And I will give grass in thy fields for thy cattle, and thou shalt eat and be satisfied.

Take heed to yourselves lest your heart be deceived, and ye turn aside and serve other gods and worship them; and the anger of the Lord be kindled against you, and he shut up the heavens, so that there shall be no rain, and the ground shall not yield its fruit, and ye perish quickly from off the good land which the Lord giveth you.

Therefore shall ye lay up these words in your heart and in your soul; and ye shall bind them for a sign upon your hand, and they shall be for frontlets between your eyes. And ye shall teach them to your children, talking of them when thou sittest in thy house, and when thou walkest by the way, and when thou liest down, and when thou risest up. And thou shalt write them upon the doorposts of thy house, and upon thy gates; that your days may be multiplied, and the days of your children, in the land which the Lord sware unto your fathers to give them, as the days of the heavens above the earth. (Deut. XI.13-21.)

And the Lord spoke unto Moses, saying: Speak unto the children of Israel, and bid them to make them fringes on the borders of their garments, throughout their generations, and put upon the fringe of each border a thread of blue; and it shall be unto you for a fringe, that ye may look upon it and remember all the commandments of the Lord and do them; and that ye follow not after your own heart and your own eyes, after which ye use to go astray; that ye may remember and do all my commandments, and be holy unto your God. *I am the Lord your God, who brought you out of the land of Egypt, to be your God; I am the Lord your God.* (Num. XV.37-41.)

III. *Geullah.*—True, steadfast, firm, enduring, right, and faithful; beloved and precious, desirable and pleasant, revered and mighty, well-ordered and acceptable, good and beautiful is this word which thou hast spoken to us from of old and for evermore.

Thou hast been the support of our fathers, their Shield and Salvation, their Deliverer and Redeemer from of old. Thou art the first and thou art the last, and beside thee we have no King, Redeemer, or Saviour: *Blessed art thou, O Lord, who redeemest Israel!*

4. *Continuity of the Liturgy with the Old Testament*

It is clear that the religious teaching of the Old Testament was completely taken for granted in the first century, not only in the Jewish practice of religion but also, and especially, in Jewish worship. The language of the prayers, familiar to every Jew from his childhood, was the very same language which he heard or read in the Psalter and in Second Isaiah. To assume, as many modern writers do, that Tannaite Judaism was a religion in decline, and that the great utterances of faith and devotion in the Old Testament Psalter and Prophets were now forgotten and meant nothing, is quite gratuitous and wholly unsupported by the evidence. A religion in decline does not produce saints and martyrs: but the Jewish religion, from the days of the early Maccabees to the death of Akiba in A.D. 135 (the period now under consideration), had a noble line of both saints and martyrs. That its ethical teaching was also on a high plane is evident from the surviving literature: from Sirach (Ecclesiasticus), from the Wisdom of Solomon, from the ethical sections in I and II Enoch, from the Testaments of the Twelve Patriarchs, from the old tradition of biblical interpretation incorporated in the Mishnah and in later Jewish writings, from the little manual for rabbinic students known as *Pirqe Aboth* (Sayings of the Fathers), and from still other sources—we may now add a few passages (not many) from the Dead Sea Scrolls.

(1) *The theology of the Psalter*, which was still in the first century the "Hymn Book of the Second Temple" and was also used in the synagogue, set forth a high conception of God the Creator (Pss. cxxxvi, cxxxix) who was revealed—that is, who revealed himself—in the powers of nature, not only in great cataclysms of storm and tempest, earthquake and volcano (Pss. xviii, xxix, cvii), but also in the orderly course of the seasons, in the moon and the stars by night and the sun by day (Pss. viii, xix, civ, cxlviii)—these were not gods, as the pagans thought, but the works of God (Gen. i, Pss. xix, lxxxix,

xcv, cxv). Equally truly, Yahweh was the God of history, as the prophets had taught (Pss. lxxviii, xc, cxiv), so that the turmoil of the nations was not beyond his control (Pss. ii, xlvi) and no assault upon his people would ultimately prevail (Pss. xlviii, cxxix). Israel he had specially chosen for himself, to be his own people (Pss. lxxx, xcix, cvf.), and he had sealed his relation with them by the establishment of his holy Covenant (Pss. xxv, lxxiv, lxxxix, cv, cxi, cxix). Though Assyria, Babylon, or Egypt might appear to dominate the world scene, their power was only human and temporary, indeed evanescent (Pss. lxviii, lxxiv, lxxix, cxxxvi). Though oppressors within the nation might tread down the pious poor, they too would fade away before the just judgment of God (Pss. xxxv, xxxvii, lii, cix). The bitter cry of the persecuted would surely be heard, and God in his faithfulness would rescue or "redeem" them (Pss. vii, xxii, xxvii, lxxii, cii). God's rule or "kingdom" is from everlasting to everlasting (Pss. xxiv, xciii, xcvif., cxlv), and the nation that feared the Lord would be vindicated in the end (Pss. ix, xl). The true expression in history of this ever-lasting rule of the Creator was the theocracy, with David (or his line, or his greater descendant still to come) as king under God (Pss. lxxii, lxxxix, cx, cxxxii) and with Aaron (or the Levitical priesthood) as his priest and minister (Pss. cxv, cxxxv). In the Dead Sea Scrolls, these are the two "anointed ones", the Messiah (or anointed king) and the anointed high priest. (Compare the Anointed from David and from Levi, in the *Testaments of the XII Patriarchs*, Levi 18.)

As everyone knows, great emphasis is laid upon personal religion in the Psalms, so great in fact that for many centuries the Psalter has been the favourite and best known Old Testament book. Such Psalms as xxii, xxx, xxxi, xxxv, and lxix are filled with a feeling of release and a certainty of restoration, both guaranteed by the power of God. Their authors have come out of the dark valley of frustration and defeat into the bright sunlight of God's presence. It is true, there is little "assurance of immortality" in the Psalms—or anywhere else in the Old Testament, aside from certain apocalyptic passages. The psalmists would seem almost to have followed the admonition of the poet:

Hath man no second life? Pitch this one high!

"The living, the living, he shall praise thee" (cf. Isa. xxxvIII.19). It was in this steady converse of devout souls with God that the deepest experiences of religion, that is, the deepest possible under the circumstances, were unfolded to them. In fact, it was out of a sublime trust in God, in spite of all outward circumstances, that the hope of a life to come eventually arose (see Dan. xII.2f.).

(2) *The theology of II Isaiah* is the loftiest and most poetic example of Jewish religious thought to be found in the Old Testament. Professor Charles Cutler Torrey called the Servant Songs "the most sublime religious poem in the world". This theology and that of the Psalter tally at almost every point: for the theology of the Psalms is expressed in a collection of hymns, old and new, which has been edited from much the same religious viewpoint as that which inspired the great anonymous prophet of the Exile. Yahweh is the only God of Israel, and he is the one true God. He is not only the God of Israel, but the Creator of the universe, for whom the whole world is but a drop in the bucket; he "taketh up the isles as a very small thing" (xL.12-31). He is the Lord of history who determines in advance the boundaries of the nations, and who decrees the fates of all people. His law, that is his will, determines all human destinies. He can foresee the future and inspire his prophets to predict it. As contrasted with the gods of the heathen, he alone is the "living" God—they are mere idols, fashioned of wood or stone (xLIV.9-20; xLVI.1-7). It is because of his loving care for Israel that he will protect his people in their exile and eventually, indeed very soon, restore them to their own land. He personally will conduct them across the desert from Babylon, when even greater miracles than those of the Exodus from Egypt will take place. His people Israel is God's "Servant", and "in all their affliction he was afflicted, and the angel of his presence saved them" (LxIII.9). The sufferings of the servant described in Chapter LIII are clearly those of the nation, though many scholars think that the picture is not only drawn from the figure of some ancient saint, but also gives in dim outline and by anticipation the portrait of the One who "bore the sins of many" on the cross. This chapter, indeed the whole series of Servant Songs, records the profoundest insight achieved by any writer of the Old

Testament into the mystery of human suffering. At its heart is a divine purpose—more than that, one can say there is a divine sharing in human pain and grief. Such a view was impossible for most ancient religions, though they had their quasi-human, semi-divine sufferers: Prometheus chained to the rock, Demeter mourning for her daughter, Attis and Osiris dying like mortals. But in the Bible it is the supreme God, the one and only God, who suffers with and for his people. The fact that Patripassianism became a Christian heresy must not blind us to the fact that God is represented in the Bible, and especially in the Old Testament, as suffering with his people. The line in *Green Pastures* is profoundly true, both of the Old Testament and of the New—being God is no "bed of roses". In this as in other respects, the New Testament conception of God is not unique, but is derived from the Old Testament conception. What is truly unique is the *biblical* conception of God, enshrined in both the Old Testament and the New.

A comparison of the old Jewish liturgy with the loftiest religious thought of the Old Testament makes it abundantly clear that ancient Judaism was a faithful "depository"—Père Bonsirven's term—of the divine revelation, and was no moribund faith, steeped in formalism, superstition, or hypocrisy, as is often assumed by ignorant and belligerent protagonists of certain types of Christianity. Modern research makes it clear likewise that the synagogue was steadily becoming the vital centre of Jewish religious life during the Tannaite period, so that even before the fall of Jerusalem and the destruction of the temple in A.D. 70 it had become the local focus of Jewish worship. The church's debt to the synagogue is also clearer now than ever before, as a result of modern research. This debt extends beyond the religious "ideology" and terminology which it shared with or inherited from the synagogue. It included the form of organisation, the titles of officers (elder or presbyter, teacher, and so on), the centrality and authority of the church in Jerusalem, the Greek Bible read at public worship and studied or expounded publicly and privately, the idea of a canon of scripture, the form and order of the service of worship ("the service of the Word"), the church's moral teaching and the technical terms in which it was set forth—in all these important aspects the church's Jewish heritage was of paramount importance. Sixty years ago it could be maintained that the church drew upon Greek political and religious organisations for its ideas of organisation and order—the assemblies (*ekklēsiai*) or the religious clubs (*thiasoi*) or the mysteries; but this view is impossible today. The line from the Jewish synagogue to the early church is far shorter and more direct. The idea that the conditions reflected in I Cor. XII-XIV, the corybantic speaking with "tongues" and all the rest of the Corinthian exuberance and indiscipline, were typical of the whole early church is preposterous: it is simply inconceivable that a congregation of sober Palestinian Christian Jews should have acted in that way. The whole New Testament stands against it—the quotations from the Old Testament and the multitude of allusions to it presuppose that the ordinary early Christian was expected to be as familiar with the scriptures as any devout member of a Jewish synagogue, who heard them read at every service.

It is against the background of these facts that the antagonism between the church and the synagogue, beginning at a very early date in Christian history, must be studied and evaluated. Much of the antagonism was personal rather than based on principle; and the effects of persecution, at first of Christians by Jews and later of Jews by Christians, have only widened into a deep gulf what originally was only a tiny fissure. One step toward a more reasonable view, if not a final reconciliation, is the recognition by Christians of the genuinely religious nature of Jewish faith, worship, and practice, all of which were—and are—centred in or inspired by the House of Prayer and Study.

5. *The Life of Prayer in Judaism*

It may of course be objected that this high, inspired "theology" of psalmist and prophet—and liturgy—was peculiar to the writers. What of the rank and file, or of the "wayfaring man" who gave little thought to such matters? But the answer must begin with another question: How are we to judge any theology—by its purest expression or by the extent to which it dominates the thinking of the ordinary man? For most

religions, it is the expression of their noblest ideas and aspirations in the familiar liturgy, catechism, hymns, lectionary,
private prayers, and popular books, or even in church windows
and statuary, that makes possible their influence upon the
rank and file.   In most religions, including Christianity, it is
the prayers men are taught to say, the sacred lections they hear
read at public worship, the hymns they sing, the catechism
they memorise, the stories they hear or read, which convey
religious truth to them—far more emphatically and concretely
than the sermons they hear, or the echoes that reach them
from the theological discourses or discussions in the schools.
And so it was in ancient Judaism.

Take the daily prayers, for example, not only those prescribed in the synagogue liturgy but also those found in that
manual of devotion which stands at the very beginning of the
great collection of Jewish legal tradition, the Mishnah, as its
first tractate, *Berakhoth*, "Blessings" (that is, benedictions,
prayers): "What is the benediction to be said over fruits?
Over tree-fruit they say: '[Blessed art thou, O Lord our God,
King of the Universe,] who createst the fruit of the tree'; over
wine, 'Who createst the fruit of the vine'; over fruits of shrubs
and bushes [literally, fruits of the earth], 'Who createst the
fruit of the ground'; over bread, 'Who bringest forth bread
from the earth' " (vɪ.ɪ).   If one sees a place where miracles
have been wrought for Israel, he must say, "Blessed be he who
wrought miracles for our fathers in this place"; or if he sees
shooting stars, earthquakes, lightnings, thunders, or storms,
he—unlike the pagans, who viewed them as portents or
prodigies—must say, "Blessed be he whose power and might
fill the whole universe" (ɪx.ɪ-2).   It may perhaps surprise
some readers to find that the Mishnah opens with a tractate
on prayer, and that the spirit of these prayers is that of simple
devotion and piety, not far removed from the spirit of an old-
fashioned Catholic or evangelical "Guide to Daily Living".
The precise definition of the prayer to be said, for example
the grace at meals when few persons are present, or when there
is a larger number, or perhaps a huge crowd, may strike us
as a bit of over-definition; but this is what any religion must
do if it sets out to provide examples of prayers for certain
occasions.   A benediction or "grace" at table when two or

three sit down to a modest lunch is scarcely the same thing as a formal invocation at a great banquet! Even the most sturdy Protestant among us must admit that the distinction is valid, at least in this case. But it is not the casuistry, which is incidental—though inevitable in any religion that prescribes rules for its adherents—it is the piety, the glowing devotion and humility of heart that breathes through these prayers, and throughout the whole treatise, that impresses us most deeply. The men who built up this system of piety through the centuries were certainly men of saintly outlook, for whom the chief end of life was to obey and adore their Father in heaven.

Not long ago I visited the University of Chicago. Walking along Fifty-seventh Street, I saw a poster announcing a lecture, to be given under the auspices of the Hillel Society, the religious organisation of the Jewish students. The subject was "The Pharisees: Saints or Hypocrites?" Without hearing the lecture, I for one am prepared to answer, "Saints", for that is certainly what the best of them were, and what most of them aspired to be.

CHAPTER FOUR

The "Theology" of
Ancient Judaism

As distinguished from popular modern Christianity, ancient
Judaism was a system of religious practice, based on the
ancient Torah, the Law code of Moses, rather than a system of
theology or of religious ideas. Certainly Judaism recognised
ideas, and based man's life upon them; but the exposition and
application of these ideas came in religious practice, not in
their purely theoretical, logical, or metaphysical coordination.
As compared with contemporary paganism, it was the purest
and loftiest religion known to the ancient world. It was this
religion which Jesus and the gospel were destined to "fulfill"
and complete, to deepen and enrich (Matt. v.17-20), and
whose foundation principles—revelation, redemption, religious
ethics, and eschatology—the church was to take over, modify,
and express in terms which the Graeco-Roman world could
understand and accept. The task was never fully accomplished
—certainly it has not been accomplished up to the present.
For the church, in the course of time, fell too greatly under
the spell of pagan rhetoric and philosophy, and tended to
substitute correct definitions of doctrine for "justice, mercy,
and the love of God". A system of piety became in time a
system of dogma—not, of course, entirely (the formula is too
sweeping), but to such an extent that to this very day Christianity is still off balance, and needs far more emphasis upon
its ethical and devotional sides, to offset the huge over-emphasis
upon doctrine which took place from the fifth to the eighth
century and again from the thirteenth to the seventeenth.

Fully realising the limitations we face, especially the non-theological nature of ancient Jewish teaching, we may nevertheless attempt to sum up the chief points of doctrine in first century Judaism, contemporary with the rise of Christianity, and presupposed by the religious thought or "theology" of the early church as it is reflected in the New Testament. This also, we shall find, is continuous with the highest religious conceptions of the Old Testament, and reflects the same religious feeling and aspiration that we find in the ancient Jewish liturgy.

1. *Monotheism*

There is only one God—only the One who is truly God. Instead of one God supreme above, or at least superior in power to all other gods—as in paganism, where Zeus was more or less *primus inter pares*—there is and can be only one God; every representation of a plurality of deities is simply false. (The stage of "henotheism", as modern scholars call it, had long been left behind in Israel's religious history.) Hence the unending ridicule of polytheism and idolatry, and the oft-repeated arguments against them, as in the prophetic and Wisdom writings. (Cf. Isa. XLIV, XLVI, Ps. CXV, and Wisd. Sol. XIII-XIV). No mere unity of "the deity" (*to theion*—the "divine" principle) under all names and appearances, no admission that the various gods were symbols or manifestations of the one God—as among cultured and philosophic pagans—was ever tolerated by Judaism. Polytheism and creature worship were too abhorrent for any compromise, too terrible in their historical consequences for toleration.

But even the purest monotheism did not rule out the recognition of subordinate spiritual beings, inferior to God as his creatures but superior to man in nature, power, knowledge, and nearness to God. They were deathless, and were endowed with supernatural abilities and knowledge, true denizens of heaven, and obedient ministers of the divine will. These were the angels, archangels, "sons of Elohim", the seven or the four spirits about the throne; or the personified "Wisdom" of Proverbs and the Wisdom of Solomon; or—viewed from some aspects—the Logos and the divine "Powers" of Philo. Certain passages in the Old Testament apparently described them as fleeting existences, comparable to winds and flames (Ps. CIV.4; cf. Heb. 1.7); but first century Judaism took for granted their permanence, if not their hypostatic or independent existence. Once having created them, God did not return them to nothingness—not even when some of them fell into sin and disobedience and became wicked spirits.

2. *The Creation*

The world was made and is sustained by the word or the will of God. It is his creation, subordinate to him, and not co-eternal or the expression of a material principle outside of and in opposition to him. Though the question was not raised, no Jew would have accepted the theory of the eternity of matter. The continuance of the world is entirely dependent upon God—the doctrine was taught in the Old Testament (e.g. Job XXXIII.4). Although the actual continuance of the world is taken for granted, even under transformed conditions, this did not confer upon matter, or "nature", an existence independent of the will of God the Creator. Judaism had already faced and rejected the dualistic hypothesis of Mazdaism.

The created world includes the whole universe, visible and invisible, land, seas, the "firmament" of heaven and the vast deeps beneath the earth, the realms of the living and the dead, the seven heavens, and the abodes of angels and spirits—even of the dead in Sheōl and the cavernous prisons of the damned.

The world was created "in the beginning"; it will end when "a new heaven and a new earth" take its place or when both are renewed or "transformed" and "become light" (as in Enoch and other apocalypses).

3. *Divine Revelation*

God has made himself known to men through the Law (Torah or Teaching), through prophets and teachers, through the Book which contains "the Torah, the Prophets, and the Writings"—and also, according to the scribes and Pharisees, through the Oral Tradition which, on their theory, accompanied the written Law (see *Pirqe Aboth* 1.1ff.). Potentially, God had revealed himself to all men; actually, it was only

Israel who "heard and obeyed" the divine Voice, and promised obedience to the divine Law (Ex. xxiv.3, 7; cf. xix.8).

There was no conception of progressive revelation; yet it was recognised that God had made himself known partially to the patriarchs (indeed, in some small measure even to the pagans—for example, through the works of nature, or the "Noachian" commandments), but more fully and more explicitly (indeed, completely) to Moses—that is, through the Torah. The prophets added no further revelation; they enforced only the teaching of the Torah, applied it to particular situations, and appealed to or warned the Israelites when they fell into sin, calling them to repentance with promises of restoration. Revelation was an unceasing process, yet complete from the beginning; for the sacred history was the story of the activity of the living God in his dealings with men, chiefly his dealings with his own people Israel. Accordingly, the Law was viewed as both oral and written; the "tradition of the elders" contained it—as did also the written Torah.

4. *The Doctrine of Election*

Israel was God's chosen people, not because of any merit of theirs but because of his boundless love and mercy (or grace). So far as merit existed on Israel's part, it was either (*a*) due to the response to the revelation at Sinai and the ancestral promise of obedience, or it was (*b*) the merit of the fathers, the patriarchs who "walked with God and pleased him". These were great ideal figures in the distant past, men upright and "perfect in God's sight", "friends of God", out of consideration for whom God dealt mercifully with their descendants, and granted them special favours (cf. Rom. xi.28).

5. *The Sacred Covenant*

The highest favour God had shown to Israel, and the highest privilege men could possibly enjoy, was the "everlasting *Berith*" (Covenant, Agreement, Promise) into which God had entered with the descendants of Abraham. Relatively to what God offered and promised, man's share in the Agreement, that is, God's demands, were few and simple: Circumcision (the badge of membership in the sacred covenant-people), Sabbath (symbol of the total consecration of man's toil and effort), Tithes (symbol of the consecration of all his possessions and "increase", that is, income, earnings, and gains), and the observance of the whole Law, positive and negative, what we call "moral" as well as what we call "ceremonial". Ancient Judaism did not distinguish between moral and ceremonial laws, or between "light" commandments and "heavy"; all were commandments of the Father in heaven. It was no cause of difficulty that some of the requirements seemed meaningless—or even absurd, like those governing cloth fabrics, birds' nests, or the cooking of goat's flesh. Enough that God had his reasons for commanding them. If an earthly father made such requests, would his sons not yield unquestioning obedience? "How much the more", then, when it was the will of the Father in heaven!

As we have already explained, Torah, at least as it was understood by the Pharisees, by the early sopherim (scribes), and by the later rabbis, meant a *rule of life*; and the Oral Tradition was only the perfectly natural casuistic elaboration and detailed application (in some cases even the modification) of that rule. Thus the Law was no burden to the pious Jew, but his "joy and crown". By giving his Torah to his own people, God was enabling them to thread successfully the strange mazes of man's pathway upon earth. These laws, as the prophet had said, were "statutes whereby a man should live and not die". (Compare Lev. xviii.15, xxv.18, xxvi.3-13; and contrast Ezek. xx.25.) Their full observance was the avowed purpose of "all Israel" after the restoration by Ezra, when Judaism became more of a church than a nation.

6. *The Problem of Sin*

Although the primitive conception of sin no doubt still survived, that is, the breach of some ceremonial taboo, or contamination with some quasi-physical pollution,[1] or obsession ("possession") by some wicked spirit, it was nevertheless generally thought of in *ethical* terms, as disobedience to the

[1] See my *How to Read the Bible*, Ch. III (New York, Morehouse, 1956; Edinburgh, Nelson, 1959).

revealed will of God. As also in the New Testament, the primitive conception of sin had now given way to the personal:

> Against thee, thee only, have I sinned,
> and done that which is evil in thy sight (Ps. LI.4).

This deeper awareness of the personal nature of sin clearly reflected the lofty teaching of the prophets and psalmists, and of prophetic-minded priests whose teaching is enshrined in parts of the Torah.

For unconscious or unintentional sin, there was a remedy (Lev. IV-V), and also the annual Day of Atonement (Ch. XVI). For conscious, intentional sins against one's neighbour, confession, restitution, and reparation were required. But for sins "with a high hand", that is, conscious, intentional sin, open defiance and direct disobedience of the explicit commands of God, carried out deliberately and with full knowledge of the consequences—what the later Christian church (following I John V.16) called "mortal" sin—there was no "place of repentance". Only the unmerited grace of God, beyond all reason or expectation, could grant forgiveness in such cases (see Ezek. XVIII, XXXIII, XXXVI). The problem of "unforgivable" sin, which rarely arose, was much the same as in the New Testament: it was "unforgivable" largely because, as a matter of fact, the sinner did not, and presumably could not, repent (cf. Mark III.28ff., Heb. VI.4-8). For him, evil was now good, and good evil, and he no longer was able to "turn" to God in penitence. (The Hebrew conception of repentance was turning, *teshubah*, away from sin and toward God.)

There is no doctrine of "original sin" in the Old Testament or in ancient Judaism—though the materials were present out of which in time the doctrine was formed. It is not man's nature that is defective, though the limitations of his finitude and mortality are clearly recognised—he, like the Egyptians' horses, is "flesh, not spirit" (Isa. XXXI.3), and consequently he must die; nor is it the "corrupt following of Adam" which accounts for human misery and wrongdoing; instead, it is the pragmatic and observable fact of wrong thinking, wrong desiring, evil habit and wicked custom that explains the widespread extent of sin and its terrible consequences (Gen. VI.5).

F

It is only in the later apocalyptic literature that we see the first beginnings of a doctrine of original sin (II Esdras VII.46-56=116-126).

7. Divine Forgiveness

God's forgiveness of human sin was believed to be abundant, unhesitating, free, and complete—and conditional only upon repentance.

(a) It was not forgiveness that "the merits (*zechuth*) of the fathers" had won for Israel, but only the generally favourable and privileged status of their descendants under the Covenant.

(b) Nor, contrary to popular modern ideas of ancient Judaism, was divine forgiveness conditional upon the offering of sacrifice, for example on the Day of Atonement.

(c) It is only in late Hellenistic works, for example II and IV Maccabees, that the deaths of the righteous are viewed as "meritorious" and somehow effective in removing the sin of the people—even here there is no suggestion that they earn or win the divine forgiveness, which is already at hand, waiting to be put in operation upon repentance. The idea seems to be rather to find some explanation, some meaning, some value, in the martyrs' deaths. If anything, Judaism erred on the side of over-emphasising the free grace of God, his infinite loving-kindness (if this be error!), and in consequence made forgiveness much too simple and too easy to obtain. Yet it must be acknowledged that the teaching of Jesus (see his story of the Prodigal Son, for example, in Luke XV.11-32) stands far closer to Judaism than it does to the teaching of St. Paul—or than the teaching of Paul stands to Judaism. For Paul, as for Gentile Christianity generally, then and since, the emphasis has been upon the *cost* of forgiveness, to God, and to Christ. "The redemption of their soul is precious" (Ps. XLIX.8 BCP); hence forgiveness must not be thought too free—the God of Israel must not be represented as weak and sentimental! (cf. Heb. XII.29).

8. Eschatology: The Goal of History

Jewish eschatology, derived directly from earlier prophecy, and consciously relying upon the prophetic oracles, was primarily national, not individual. That is, it arose out of concern for the welfare, the survival, the future safety and salvation (not to say victory and triumph) of the group, threatened with extinction in a barbarous and unfriendly world. It even went the length of a jingoistic dream of world dominion—as in Isa. LX and Dan. VII. Hence the great revival of eschatological interest and emphasis, now under the guise of apocalyptic (that is, books of secret revelation) rather than of prophecy, which took place from early Maccabean days onward for three centuries and more.

It was out of this "national" or "social" (that is, "group") expectation that the individual eschatology arose. The first clear expectation of individual resurrection is found in Daniel XII.2f. (c. 165 B.C.) and in probably contemporary psalms and apocalyptic fragments, some of them now found embedded in the writings of the prophets. Whether or not, as some hold, this doctrine owed its formulation to Mazdean (that is, Zoroastrian) influence, its actual rise in Israel was the result of the crisis in the days of Antiochus IV. Hellenistic Judaism knew the doctrine of resurrection only as derived from Palestinian teaching; the normal Greek conception was that of the immortality of the soul. (See Wisdom III.1-9.) Paul combined the two, more or less, in his doctrine of the "spiritual" body. Similar views are found in some of the apocalypses.

The various details of this hope, as held by many different writers, believers, scholars, and saints, will be set forth in the next chapter. For the moment, we may pause and look back to the massive, immovable convictions upon which ancient Judaism rested. Israel's God is the one, true, and only God, the Creator and Sustainer of the universe, the Father and lover of mankind. His gracious self-revelation has taken place both in nature and in history and above all in the words of prophets and teachers, in the characters of holy and faithful men and women, in the lives of his servants and saints. This process of revelation included the choice of certain persons, families, peoples to be the receivers of his revelation and the bearers of his gracious good will toward all mankind; this is clear both from the sacred history and from mature reflection upon human experience in general. But such special choices imply not only special privileges but also special responsibilities: "From those to whom much is given, much will be required" (cf. Luke XII.48b). God of his own will and for his own purposes had chosen Israel to be his "slave"—our English word "servant" greatly softens the idea—his messenger and agent in the divine economy. Thus the unilateral "Covenant" or "Agreement" was made with Israel, involving Israel in a life of obedience to the divine law in all its detailed requirements, for Israel's good, but *not* as the result of Israel's special deserving. Salvation is by divine grace, as much in the Old Testament as in the New!

Chiefly, this Covenant provided for the maintenance of a *state* of grace, whereby Israel as a people could continue to enjoy the divine favour; hence provision was made to secure the removal of sin, both its dangerous pollution (the primitive conception) and also its inexcusable guilt (the later prophetic conception). Divine forgiveness was not procured by the offering of sacrifices—God forgives man at once upon repentance. What the sacrifices effected was something deeply laid in "primitive" social and religious tradition, and derived from conditions long antedating recorded history.[1] Hence the "sacrificial system" was also primitive, much of it connected with prehistoric taboos—as was also the case in the ancient Greek and Roman religions, and many others. The ritual was definitely prescribed, but the "reason why"—this no one knew; perhaps no one had ever known, for the practices of ancient religion, including the Hebrew, were often derived from stages of religious development long antedating logical analysis or theory. These things were done just because they always had been done, and because they always worked! This was reason enough for most religious men in the ancient world. Of course, it would never have produced a theology.

Finally, as the corollary and climax to the whole religious *Weltanschauung* of ancient Judaism, God the Creator must carry through his purposes to their final conclusion; God the Wise and Good, God the One who had chosen Israel to be his Servant, must finally see his world in its finished, perfect state, not frustrated or wrecked by human sin or demonic evil. Hence the really optimistic conviction prevails that evil is only temporary and must eventually be overcome; hence also the straight-line conception of history prevails, as opposed to the

---

[1] See § 6, above, and the reference in the footnote there.

pagan theory of cyclical recurrence—for history is going somewhere, an arrow to the target, a highway to its destination, as "God is working his purpose out". Ancient Jewish thought, like ancient Christian, was "eschatological" from beginning to end, for it took account of the divine overruling of events, and saw all history, both past and present, in the light of God's ultimate purpose. And that purpose was good, not evil—such trust had the Jew in his God—and its final goal was *shalōm*, peace, salvation, blessedness.

Modern research has shown that the basic doctrines or tenets of ancient Judaism were presupposed by the early Christians. Monotheism, the divine revelation, the sacred history, even the idea of the Covenant were all taken over by the early church and reinterpreted. But the reinterpretation presupposed the reality and validity of the earlier teaching. The sacrificial system was rejected—but it was already about to pass away (Heb. IX.12), and in fact did cease in A.D. 70. The legalistic, scribal interpretation of the Law was rejected, beginning with Paul, even with Jesus and the primitive church in Jerusalem (see Acts VI-VII), but its deep underlying principles, the eternal foundations of the moral order—these are as fully taken for granted by Paul, the Hellenists, and the Gentile Christians as by any Palestinian Christian or Jewish inter-preters of the sacred Torah (see Matt. v.17-20). When the theology of the New Testament is described as "a Jewish theology in transition" (see p. xi), this is what is meant: the basic principles of the older religious teaching are presupposed, modified, and given a new centre and emphasis. The basis of New Testament theology is not Greek philosophy, either Platonism or Stoicism; nor is it "Oriental mysticism", so popular in the historical writings of fifty years ago; it is Judaism. This is the rock from whence it sprang, this is the aged mother from whom it was born. *Antiquam exquirite matrem!*

CHAPTER FIVE

The Messianic Hope

Nothing is more characteristic of Jewish eschatology than its variety; it was anything but a "system", and there is no consistency in details. There were no dogmas in Judaism, and each individual was free to work out his own theology or theodicy if and as he desired; moreover, various types of religious experience lie behind the varieties of eschatological thought, some more biblical, some less, some visionary and apocalyptic, some prophetic or reflective.

1. *"The Time of the End"*

A constantly pressing question was asked repeatedly, "*When* will the end come?" This was variously answered, upon the basis of scripture and by other computations. In times of acute distress, seers and apocalyptic writers tended to think the end near at hand; at other times it apparently receded. The same had been true in Old Testament days, and it was true also in New Testament times, and in later church history as well.

Another question was this, "Could men by their deeds or their prayers *hasten* the coming of the end?" In answer, the time was said to be fixed, and the end could not come until this time had been completed (or "fulfilled"), or until the measure of evil was "full", or the number of the elect. The time is wholly in God's hands (Acts 1.8); he alone determines it, he alone knows what it is. And though "for the elect's sake" he may "shorten the days" (see p. 90), or in the interest of repentance may extend the interval of grace, still it is he alone who does this—and no human being can alter or modify his decree.

Some writers tried to compute "the time of the end" mathematically, assuming that history advances by a pre-determined schedule of successive ages, ever moving toward the climax which God has set as its goal. On the other hand, certain writers insisted that such attempts at calculation were incompatible with trust in God, and therefore forbade them, teaching that men must humbly acknowledge their ignorance and wait patiently for God to act. (The teaching of Jesus and the New Testament as a whole support this latter view.)

Nevertheless, it was agreed, chiefly on the basis of Old Testament prophecy, the end would be preceded by various warning signs. Chief among these was the expected "time of tribulation" foretold by the prophets. This was to be a period of terrible persecution and distress for the Jewish people. The evil world powers (or power) would attack the people of God, and once more Jerusalem would be besieged. The details of this anticipated final onslaught upon Jerusalem go back at least to the great apocalyptic vision of Gog and Magog in Ezekiel xxxviii-xxxix, where the successive stages of the attack are described and also the miraculous destruction of the invaders.

But it was also thought that the time of tribulation would involve the whole world, and not just Palestine. Evil, wickedness, and sin would gain the upper hand or would outweigh righteousness, and the consequences even for the physical world would begin to be disastrous. Chaos would break out in heaven and the stars would either fall from the skies or move erratically off their courses. All nature would begin to be upset, prodigies would appear, famine and plague would become more common, the life of men would grow shorter, disease would spread, the mass of men would go down to destruction, and only a remnant would survive. As in modern millenarian theory, which is directly derived from ancient Jewish apocalyptic, when the need grows most desperate the end will come.

The motivation of this eschatological theory was partly exegetical, partly theological. It was the expectation of men who looked longingly for the divine reign, but who felt in their

heart of hearts that it could not come to pass until wickedness
had been allowed a final fling. It also reflects, undoubtedly,
the social psychology of Judaism, repressed and obstructed
by other nations and by the growing world imperialism of
Rome, experiencing repeated persecutions, and threatened
continually with annihilation, and yet hoping and trusting
that in the end God would vindicate his own people.

The idea of a "Day of the Lord" goes back a long way in
Judaism and in the earlier Hebrew religion. Before the time
of Amos in the eighth century B.C., it was assumed that "the
Day of the Lord" would usher in a marvellous era of peace
and prosperity. But Amos insisted that this Day would be
"darkness, not light" (Amos v.18). God would not overlook
the evil of the world, or the sins of men, when he visited the
earth—nor would he overlook the sins of Israel. From the
time of Amos, apparently, it was assumed that "the Day of
the Lord" would be a "Day of Judgment" or of "Visitation".
The term has many synonyms in the later prophets. The idea
is present in much of the Old Testament and is a commonplace in apocalyptic; it is also found in much of the other
ancient Jewish literature. Apparently it was one of the basic
conceptions of early Judaism.

2. The Coming Messiah

During this "last evil time", which was to precede the end
of the present age, a number of persons were expected to
return: certain of the prophets, or at least one of them—say
Moses, or Elijah (Mal. iv.5), or the "witness" in Fourth Ezra,
1 Enoch, and the Apocalypse of John (where there are two,
Rev. xi.3). Moreover, angels were expected to come to
earth, as forerunners of the Messiah. This expectation of
returning heavenly or historical personages is also reflected
in the New Testament. John the Baptist was looked upon
by many as the "Elijah who is to come", or possibly (on one
interpretation) as Jeremiah, or at least as one of the ancient
prophets come back again. Similar speculations circulated
regarding Jesus himself. (See John 1.19-23; Mark ix.13,
vi.14-16, viii.27f.)

One of the commonest elements in the biblical eschatology
was the expectation of the messianic King, that is, God's

Anointed, who is to reign in the Age to Come. It runs through-out much of the apocalyptic literature and is found in many of these books, though not in all; it is also found in the Jewish liturgy (see p. 47) and in the oldest of the rabbinic writings, in the Dead Sea Scrolls, and likewise in the Hellenistic Jewish writings. Moreover, it was a widespread popular expectation which led to repeated revolts and disturbances, until it was suppressed, though not finally, in the second century. "Messiah", of course, means "Anointed". It was the term applied to every ancient Israelite king in order to emphasise the sacred nature of his office and his supernatural equipment for his task. The great king of the Age to Come was to be supremely *the* Anointed, even though he also bore such peculiarly antiquarian or nationalistic titles as "Son of David", "the Prince", and so on. The actual term "The Messiah", with its full eschatological meaning, is not found in the Old Testament, and in the New Testament only in John 1.41, IV.25; but it is fairly common in the post-biblical literature. There it always means the glorious future king of Israel in the Age to Come. At the same time there were "messianic" dreams in which no Messiah was either included or implied—God himself would be Israel's Redeemer and King.

A wholly different type of expectation is reflected in the title "Son of Man". It is found in that section of the apocalyptic literature which apparently was more strongly influenced by Persian or Babylonian ideas, and in which the peculiarly nationalistic messianic expectation had given way to a completely supernaturalistic and celestial conception.

The point of contact between these two ideal figures was found in the quasi-divine nature of the Messiah, and in the exalted titles given to him—as to other ideal kings in the ancient Orient; it also lay in the close relation of both to the people of Israel. Thus in the Age to Come (*a*) all Israel was to be "saved" and enjoy the reign of the messianic king (Ps. Sol., XVII); or (*b*) the pious, the faithful, or the "elect" would "dwell with that Son of Man" in a glorified, supernatural condition of endless bliss (I Enoch XLVIII-LI, LXII). Common to both of these expectations—the earthly Messiah and the supernatural Son of Man—is (*c*) the pre-existence of his name and the

supernatural accompaniments of his appearance or "manifestation to Israel". He may be a returning Jewish king (David,
or a son of David), or he may be the celestial, pre-existent Son
of Man who is to come on the clouds of heaven—but in either
case he will come suddenly and unannounced, save for certain
preliminary signs of his arrival, and he will either hold the
Last Judgment (as Son of Man) or he will destroy the enemies
of Israel (as king of the elect nation).   He will also act as
judge or ruler of Israel—or of the nations.   He will bring
salvation—for Israel, and perhaps also for the few to be saved
from among the nations.

It is characteristic of ancient Oriental thought and language
that rulers, even earthly rulers, were described in transcendental
terms approaching the titles given to gods.   This is one reason
why, in the New Testament and the apocalyptic writings, no
sharp distinction is drawn between the "earthly" Messiah and
the "heavenly" Son of Man, though the two figures were
distinct in origin, and were quite differently conceived in
nature and office.   The Messiah is to be so completely a
manifestation of God that some of the religious titles and
attributes of God are transferred to him: he will be righteous,
he will possess wisdom and power, and yet at the same time
he will be filled with the fear of God.   Similarly his work will
be supernatural, almost divine, so that what he does will be
perfectly just and right; indeed, it will be what God does
through him.   He is not so much a person as an agent, not so
much an individual as a symbol of the power and the goodness
of God.   As Paul Volz once put it, he is "the personal x of the
coming era of salvation".

Various ideas were held about the date of his coming, the
length of his reign, the extent of his dominion, and the final
conclusion of his rule.   Some thought that it would last forever,
others that it would be limited to a generation, or perhaps to
four hundred years, or possibly it would extend to a thousand
—this latter idea is reflected in the Apocalypse of John (Rev.
xx.6).   It was also thought that there would be certain
stages preliminary to his coming—the rabbis spoke of
his dimly perceptible but steadily approaching footfall
("the footsteps of the Messiah") as the days of his advent drew
near.

The idea of a violent death of the Messiah, or of the sufferings of the Messiah (or of *a* Messiah) arose later than the period of the New Testament. It resulted from the identification of the Messiah with the nation of Israel, combined with the further identification of the nation of Israel with the suffering Servant of the Lord described in II Isaiah. Despite a popular modern hypothesis, there is no adequate evidence that the suffering Messiah found a place in Jewish expectation during the first century.

3. *The Resurrection*

The resurrection was either to precede, accompany, or follow the messianic era. It was to be a resurrection either of the martyrs, or of the righteous, or of all men. Various forms of the expectation are reflected in the literature: (*a*) If only the martyrs are to rise from the dead, it is because God in a sense owes it to them—they have laid down their lives in the battle, and must they not be present at the triumph? Men cannot claim this as their right; but God is just, and he will see that his servants are justly rewarded. (*b*) If all the righteous are to rise, it is for the same reason—the righteous have served God faithfully and cannot be allowed to perish, or to remain permanently in the dim and chilly halls of Sheōl (Hades). (*c*) If good and bad alike are to be raised, it is so that the former may be rewarded and the latter punished. God will not allow the wicked to escape their just penalties by an easy lapse into unconsciousness or extinction. Thus the religious motivation of the resurrection-hope, rather than any purely speculative interest, is clear wherever it appears in the older apocalyptic literature.

The departed are to rise up at the command of God, either out of their graves or out of the *promptuaria* or storerooms of souls (II Esdras IV.41). Considerable variety is found in the conception of the resurrection body. (*a*) Some believed that it would be simply a reanimation of the buried corpse, the bones acquiring a covering of flesh once more (as in Ezek. XXXVII), and severed parts of the body being restored each to its proper place. (*b*) Others held, apparently, that the soul itself would need to be reanimated. Underlying this conception is the old, really primitive idea of the soul as a faint, ethereal copy of the body, both lifeless and powerless, not at all the Platonic philosophic conception of the soul as the centre of power, vitality, and even intelligence. (c) Still others thought of the resurrection body as entirely new, comparable to fresh garments, prepared by God and given by him to deserving souls. (It is apparently with the third of these views that Paul's conception has the closest affinity—see I Cor. xv, II Cor. v.1-10.) Quite obviously, the variety in these views of the resurrection reflects a variety in anthropological conceptions. The date of the resurrection and the precise point at which it was to be included in the eschatological drama was also subject to various interpretations or speculations.

4. *The Judgment*

The Final Judgment is, of course, the essential feature in this whole expectation. The world must be brought to time, the wicked must be checked finally and forever, and the righteous must receive their reward. The world as it is cannot be allowed to go on forever; while the perfect world, the true theocracy, the Kingdom of God, his perfect Reign, cannot—God being God and therefore supreme—go forever unrealised. It is unquestionably true that God's Reign has always existed, and is "from everlasting to everlasting" (cf. Ps. CXLV.13; CIII.17-19); and yet within the divine realm, and under this divine Reign, there has been revolt, disobedience, sin, and its consequences. All this must eventually be done away, and the divine rule be established everywhere. It is in this sense that the Kingdom of God must "come", here in this present evil world: and its coming involves, inevitably, a divine judgment upon sinners and their sins.

There are, of course, many expressions of this thought of divine judgment in the Old Testament; but as in the Old Testament so also in the apocalyptic and rabbinic literature there is great variety. Sometimes the judgment is to take place here upon earth, sometimes in heaven; sometimes it is thought that it will take place at the end of the Messianic era, at other times it will precede it; some writers assume that God will be the judge, others that it will be the Messiah, or the Son of Man, or the righteous.

Various conceptions and detailed pictures of God's coming in judgment had survived from much earlier times and were still common in Jewish apocalyptic. God arrives surrounded by his hosts of angels, as in the ancient descriptions of his theophanies (for example, Deut. xxxiii.2; Ps. ciii.20f.; civ.4); and as he draws near, the signs of his presence become visible, the mountains smoke, the earth trembles, the stars fall from heaven, and sinners are filled with anguish. Sometimes, on the other hand, the scene is pictured in equally vivid ways but as a reflection of earthly courts. Sometimes the judge delivers an address; charges are formally presented by accusers; witnesses are called; the books are opened; or the judge compels the accused to condemn or exculpate themselves—all these are features that reflect earthly courts. Nothing can save the godless when they fall into the hands of the just and eternal Judge. The righteous escape, but the sinners are caught and condemned to penalties which are either ever-lasting or continue for a long time.

The Day of Judgment is of course the "last" day; there is no further "room for repentance". Whatever has been done on earth is now "over and finished", and men must forthwith give account for every word spoken, every deed performed—or left undone—throughout their whole lives. When the verdict has been decided, it is announced publicly and there is no appeal from the decision of the final Judge. Both the penalties and the rewards are permanent. Part of the penalty of the condemned (so it is suggested in one or two passages) is to look up and see the righteous in bliss; by a natural corollary, part of the bliss of heaven is to look down and see the tortures of the damned (cf. Luke xvi.19-31), an idea which unfortunately made a wide appeal and survived for many centuries. We can trace it in the Apocalypse of Peter, in Dante, and in the whole medieval conception of heaven and hell.

There was little thought of a total destruction of the wicked, though some persons speculated in this direction. Penalties were either "age-long" or endless. "Destruction" was not equivalent to annihilation. There was little thought of any remedial value in punishment; the wicked were to get their just deserts and there was no further thought beyond that point. Gradually, however, the idea suggested itself that punishment might taper off into final extinction, although, ethically viewed, punishment seemed preferable to extinction. Otherwise, the hardened sinners would get off too easily, enjoying their evil behaviour in this life and escaping full retribution in the next! Where, on the other hand, the thought of final extinction does obtain, there is a further question as to the one who shall carry it out—it is either God, or the Messiah, an angel or angels, or Israel, or the righteous, or the nations. The medium through which extinction will take place is also variously conceived. It may be through warfare, earthly or heavenly, or through the powers of nature—for example, by fire and sword, or by lightning, earthquake, pestilence, or famine; or it may be through some sudden mania or madness spread by demons, or as the inevitable final state of mind of those who all their lives long have rejected God and the counsels of obedience.

The state of the damned—a condition falling somewhat short of final extinction, or a state prior to their extinction—was likewise variously conceived. Some writers emphasised the spiritual nature of the punishments, others the physical torments involved. Darkness, flame, blindness, pain—these were features borrowed from the lurid scene south of Jerusalem where the ancient Vale of Hinnom (New Testament "Gehenna") was now the city garbage dump, with its "perpetual burnings", and also the place where the corpses of criminals were left. Others thought of "hell" as the realm of the dead beneath the earth; it was also the current Graeco-Roman idea; it was thought to include various regions or compartments, with many different types of torture—as in Virgil and Dante. It was a question whether or not hell had existed before the creation of the world. An affirmative answer involved a completely deterministic view of God's relation to the world: if he had foreseen everything, then he must also have willed it; that is to say, he had predestined it for a specific purpose and use. The next step, as in rigid Calvinism, was the utterly abhorrent one that God had predestined some men to eternal damnation.

Not only were individuals to be judged, but all the evils in the world were to be undone and put out of the way. Demons were to be judged as well as men, "and those who have led the world astray" (1 Enoch LXIX.27). Idolatry and sin—that is, breaches of the Mosaic Law—will be the special object of divine vengeance. Since the world itself is now entirely corrupt—at least it is thoroughly "infected" with corruption, on the apocalyptic view (cf. Rom. VIII.19-23)— there is nothing that can be salvaged, and so it must all be destroyed and pass away. The stars will be destroyed, the world will be burned up (an interesting contact with Stoicism; cf. II Peter III.10), the seas will boil away, the mountains will sink into the abyss—imagination could scarcely picture the terrors attending this ultimate collapse of the universe. Somehow, somewhere, the blessed were to gather as on a reviewing stand and witness the ghastly spectacle.

5. *The Age to Come*

Following the destruction of the present world, there will be (according to those who held the transcendental type of eschatology) the renewal of the world or the creation of a new one—even the stars in the heavens were to be either renewed or replaced with better ones. Though there were antecedents of this view in Old Testament prophecy, the enormous elaboration of the hope was the work of the later apocalyptists. The next step, following this world renewal, would be the revelation of God's Kingdom or Reign throughout the whole universe. Even though it already exists (as in Ps. CXLV), it exists in secret and must be "manifested" or "revealed". Though God's Reign is "from everlasting", without beginning or end, those parts of the universe which have been the scene of revolt against the divine sovereignty must be forcibly reconquered, and the rebellious provinces reincorporated once more within the empire of the divine will. It is after this has taken place, at the Last Judgment, that God's everlasting rule will be "manifested", "established", or "revealed".

Various poetic conceptions of the "coming" of God's Reign clustered about the idea. It was an age-old concept, basic to all Old Testament and Jewish thought, which was fundamentally theocratic and teleological. God will be the ruler of all the world; his glory will become visible; the whole cosmos will unite in praising him; he only will be ruler upon earth; he will be the God of all mankind. As at the beginning of the world, so at the end, there will be one God and one only, worshipped everywhere. Sinners, if not destroyed or sent to hell, will be converted and will acknowledge the divine sovereignty. The heathen will be converted and will turn to the Lord, bringing gifts to his temple—which will now become the universal temple of Israel's God, the sole temple of the true God in all the world; and the Torah will become the law of all mankind. Here we may see a contact between apocalyptic thought and the far-flung missionary efforts of Judaism in the Graeco-Roman world.

Participation in the national salvation was thought of under various terms. "Blessedness", "salvation", and "life" meant more or less the same thing. As in the gospels, to "enter into life", to "receive everlasting life", to "receive" or to "enter" the Kingdom of God meant one and the same thing, namely, final salvation. If the coming era of salvation was thought of in supernatural terms, it still gave special preference and privilege to the Jews—or at least to the pious among them. One common feature of the expectation was the return of the Diaspora or Dispersion, especially of the Lost Ten Tribes, who will stream back to Palestine from all quarters of the earth, and will be restored to their own land, while the wicked and sinners will be driven out of it, since it is a holy land. What to do with godless Israelites was a problem; an even more serious one was what to do with their little children, who as Jews were certainly entitled to share the national bliss, but who as children of the godless would probably also grow up to be ungodly. Various solutions of these problems were found, but none that was wholly satisfactory.

Those who were to enjoy the salvation were sometimes described as the righteous, sometimes as Israel, sometimes as the elect. There is no systematic theology here, but only the variety which springs out of ardent piety faced with problems. There was a similar variety in the answers to the question, Who is the righteous man? Some said it was the Jew who observed the Law; others (as in the Psalms) that it was the person who loved and obeyed God—probably more or less the same person was meant in each case. As there is now a blessed society upon earth, so there will be in heaven—or upon the renewed earth. One of the chief sources of bliss will be the reunion with those of former generations, and the great joy of living forever in the presence of the patriarchs, the prophets, and the saints. At the same time Israel will see its former persecutors and oppressors fitly punished, and the nations which have reviled Israel or which have flouted the will of God will be "destroyed".

Thus there were many different conceptions of salvation: it is "glory", it is "life", it is "length of days", it is participation in "salvation" (conceived socially or nationally), it is a whole complex of bliss, temporal and eternal, it is eternal blessedness, and it is even thought of as an endless banquet. Where the idea of the Kingdom of Israel is retained, it also is thought of in transcendental terms, not only as a state of release from servitude and oppression, but as one of positive glorification. Jerusalem will be beautified and adorned as befits the City of God. It will be built up forever, it will be enlarged, it may even in fact disappear and give place to the heavenly Jerusalem, which will descend out of the skies where it has been kept by God for the end of the world (see Rev. xxi). The temple cult will presumably continue, even in the glorified earthly Israel. The people of Israel will be greatly increased in numbers, will be completely independent, and will serve God without let or hindrance, worshipping him in accordance with his own prescribed ways as set forth in the Law, and thus achieving at last the fulfilment of the age-old dream of the theocracy.

Another feature of the era of salvation will be universal peace upon earth, as well as in Israel. There will be concord among the nations, and even in the animal kingdom—as the prophets had foretold. There also will be an inner peace in the hearts of men, and there will be an everlasting Sabbath for rest, worship, and rejoicing upon earth. Since physical evil is the consequence of sin, all earthly evils will cease when sin is no more. Furthermore, death will come to an end since death is an anomaly in God's world and is found here only because man has sinned (cf. 1 Cor. xv.26). As viewed by some writers, the bliss of the redeemed will include some very concrete terrestrial enjoyments—a greatly increased fruitfulness

G

of the soil, of herds and flocks, and even of human beings; the food of the blessed will be manna, or the flesh of Leviathan or Behemoth, or the fruit of the tree of life; children will be born without pain, and will be in perfect health; there will be no fatigue and no disease, and nothing to shorten or burden men's days. It is obvious that the writers' imaginations ran riot over the prospect; it is equally obvious that their ideas were anything but systematic, and that no theological dogmas, or even any formal doctrine, had been set up as a fixed norm to check or to control their extravagant fancies.

Since sin will disappear, there will be nothing left for Satan, the "tempter" or the "accuser", to do, and he likewise will disappear. Goodness will be triumphant, God will shower his people with spiritual gifts, and the generation of those who live upon earth will be completely pleasing to him. Men will enjoy fellowship with God, who will dwell among them and be their God (Rev. xxi.3, cf. Isa. vii.14, viii.8), and they will see his glory. The bodies of the redeemed will be fashioned out of "light", like angels, with a "body" of "glory"; they will be brighter than the stars; and they will either live forever or at least to patriarchal old age and then die painless deaths. This raises once more the question of the duration of bliss, parallel to that of the duration of punishment. Various answers were given, Jewish thought on the whole tending either to leave the question unanswered or answered only with a vague and indefinite expectation of continuity, or else with a round affirmation of eternal life.

The place of the blessed is either Jerusalem or the New Jerusalem, Palestine or the glorified Palestine of the future, Paradise, the Garden of Eden, or Heaven. Different writers conceived the place and the state of the blessed in different ways; this is a characteristic of religious eschatology the world over, and not just of Jewish apocalyptic. Even within the Catholic and Muslim eschatologies there is considerable variety, and when uniformity has been forced upon the doctrine, and a systematic statement has been demanded of it, there is still contrast, there is still variety. An example may be seen in the Catholic conception of Purgatory with its twofold penalties— the penalty of deprivation, separation from God (*poena damni*) and the penalty of fire (*poena sensus*), the one a highly spiritual conception, the other very primitive and concrete and requiring allegorical interpretation. The same is true of eternal bliss. Some ancient writers conceive it in exalted spiritual terms ("his servants shall serve him", Rev. XXII.3; or as the Beatific Vision of God, Matt. v.8); others conceive it as a mere escape from damnation or a state of egoistic satisfaction with one's own virtues. We should like to be able to say that the spiritual conception is always uppermost, and always triumphs at the end of any religious development. Unfortunately, we cannot. We can only say that there is always variety; and we are thankful to add that this was true of ancient Jewish apocalyptic, for it means that even within the somewhat barbaric and certainly bizarre variety of ancient Jewish expectation there was a genuinely spiritual element.

From such a catalogue of expectations as the preceding detailed list, it is clear that there was little uniformity in the apocalyptic dreams. The messianic hope was a kind of wishing well, with many of the wishes written down—or a Santa Claus mailbag. There was no end of variety. Some features were derived from repeated reading and pondering of the Old Testament, some from private fancies or visionary experiences, some from the antique dream of a coming golden age which was shared with other peoples in the ancient Near East. Some of the writers took a word or a phrase of the Old Testament and twisted it into a feature far more concrete or specific than the original author had intended. It is also obvious that this total mixture of aspirations, old and new, spiritual and material, religious and secular, was not really characteristic of Judaism as a whole, but grew up on the fringes of that ancient religion of cultus and practice. It was doubtless a mark of the vitality of Judaism that it produced such hopes; but they were never the main content of that religion—not by a long, long way. No doubt the apocalyptists —or most of them—were pious men; but they were not the typical saints or "pious men" of the ancient Palestinian synagogue. There are many pious British Israelites; but would anyone claim that they are typical of English-speaking Christianity? No more were the ancient Jewish apocalyptists typical of ancient Judaism.

The assumption that all first century Jews were familiar with the apocalyptic writings, or were ardent messianists, has vitiated altogether too much New Testament interpretation, especially of the gospels, ever since the beginning of the present century, largely as a result of the influence of such famous scholars as Albert Schweitzer, Alfred Loisy, Wilhelm Bousset, and R. H. Charles. And yet there is no question that the early church arose within a matrix of ardent apocalyptic expectation. Jesus himself was probably not an apocalyptist; as many now hold, his mission was prophetic, and he looked upon himself as a prophet. This view is supported by much of the oldest material in the gospels. The tendency—evident elsewhere in the New Testament—to exalt him to messianic dignity, or to the status of the transcendent Son of Man (not identical with the Messiah), was partly due to the effort to outbid Judaism, and to offset the inference which the world in general drew from the fact of his crucifixion. The psychological process by which this became virtually inevitable is now quite clear.

Although Jesus himself was probably, as we have said, not an apocalyptist, his disciples soon came under the influence of such views, which increasingly affected the whole gospel tradition during the first and second generations. Paul was steeped in it. So was the author of Revelation, the "Apocalypse of John". So were those who handed down the "Q" tradition in the gospels. So was Mark, and before Mark the author of the "Little Apocalypse", the remains of which lie embedded in Mark's Chapter XIII. One of the earliest conceptions of the exalted Christ was the "Son of Man"—a title which had far-reaching influence upon the later development of Christology. It follows, then, that the earliest church was a kind of "fringe group" in first century Judaism, and from the beginning held a view of Judaism as a whole which was much influenced by its own special interests. Hence any study of the relations between the early church and ancient Judaism must pay unusual attention to this whole area of thought. The apocalyptic element in the New Testament is only a relatively small sample of the total quantity of apocalyptic writing, both Jewish and Christian. As we shall see, it shares the same characteristics as earlier Jewish and later Christian apocalypses.

Hence it must not be judged independently of the total religious-literary phenomenon known as "apocalyptic", nor viewed more seriously than it deserves, that is, more seriously than other and similar works. The inclusion of Daniel in the Jewish canon and of the Apocalypse of John in the Christian were little more than accidental. Many other apocalypses might well have been considered. As a matter of fact IV Ezra is included in the Vulgate Bible (in the appendix) and in the English Apocrypha (as II Esdras), while the Apocalypse of Peter was viewed as scripture for a long time in certain parts of the Eastern Church. For the purposes of historical research these books are very important; they throw an immense light upon the thought and aspiration of those who handed down the gospel tradition and treasured the letters of Paul, and who preached the Christian message during the first two centuries. But they can scarcely provide data for Systematic Theology, or explain the deepest loyalties and convictions of the early Christians. By the time of Origen, apocalyptic had virtually faded out of recognition. In the earliest doctrinal expositions of the church fathers, the term "Son of Man" describes Jesus' human nature, "Son of God" his divine—an almost diametrical inversion of the original connotations of the two titles. (See Ignatius, *Ephesians* xx.2; Barnabas xii.10.)

Here lies the crucial problem for all present-day New Testament research. To what degree or in what way did Jewish apocalyptic contribute a permanent element in Christian teaching? How important was it in the formulation not only of the Christian tradition of Jesus' life and teaching and the earliest beginnings of the church, but also of the central doctrines of the Christian faith? Was Jesus the Jewish Messiah, or not? And did he think of himself as the Messiah, or the "Son of Man", or the coming King of the New Age? These questions cannot be answered without first of all taking fully into account the place of apocalyptic messianism in the Jewish religion, and then its place in the nascent Christian church. Whatever its importance, it scarcely belonged to the *essence* of either ancient Judaism or early Christianity.

Modern research has demonstrated that the messianic hope was one characteristic expression of Jewish religious faith, but that it had no uniform structure or dogmatic authorisation. It was based fundamentally on the Old Testament, with its eschatological view of history, its teleology, its unfulfilled promises of a glorious future which stood out in ever stronger contrast with the increasing difficulties and disasters which Israel faced in its actual history, from the Exile onward. That it strongly influenced early Christianity and in fact conditioned its rise does not prove that Judaism as a whole was oriented in this direction. But it enables us somewhat better to understand the shift in emphasis which Christianity represented, and the consequent tensions between Jews and Christians, especially in their interpretation of the Old Testament and their view of the future destiny of Israel (cf. Rom. ix-xi). The anti-Jewish slant given the messianic hope in the early church (especially in the Synoptic Apocalypse—that is, Mark xiii, Luke xxi, Matt. xxiv-xxv—in i and ii Thess., and in the Apocalypse of John) was a natural and perhaps necessary polemical reinterpretation and re-emphasis of the traditional eschatology; but its origin in controversy and even in mutual recrimination does not make it any sounder a basis for Christian faith or teaching. In fact, despite its unquestionable importance for an understanding of Christian origins and the earliest development of the Christian church, there are many Christians today, including some theologians, who would gladly be rid of the burden of any further maintenance of the quasi-political, purely mundane eschatology rooted in ancient Jewish messianism. Many of the Jewish leaders had themselves repudiated it by the middle of the second century, after the two disastrous and disillusioning wars against Rome ending in A.D. 70 and A.D 135. And the church had virtually repudiated it by the end of the second century.

CHAPTER SIX

Characteristic Features
of Jewish Apocalyptic

The research of the past fifty years has demonstrated that the special "seed plot" of the earliest Palestinian Christianity was the apocalyptic hope. Jesus himself was probably not an apocalyptist, and he repudiated the attempt to define the precise day and hour of the coming end of the age (cf. Mark XIII.32, Acts 1.7). Nor did he rely upon visions, dreams, or esoteric interpretations of scripture. (Many scholars now view Mark XIII and the parallel chapters in Matthew and Luke as based upon a "Little Apocalypse" of Jewish or Jewish-Christian origin, from about A.D. 40, and not originally a part of the tradition of Jesus' teachings.) Yet his followers were certainly soon influenced by this circle of ideas, and in increasing measure, apparently, within the Palestinian milieu. The doctrine of the Son of Man was developed under the influence of ideas either identical with or very similar to those found in the Book of Enoch. The expectation of the Parousia and Judgment was likewise apocalyptic in origin; that is, it was drawn from the apocalyptic rewriting of the old prophetic expectation. The place held by apocalyptic in the "modern religious literature" of first century Judaism will be clear from the accompanying table (pp. 86f.).

1. *Two Terms To Be Distinguished*

The terms "apocalyptic" and "eschatological" are sometimes used interchangeably; but this is a mistake. All Hebrew,

Apocalyptic Literature

B.C.	
587-350	Ezekiel XXXVIII-XXXIX
520-518	Zechariah I-VIII
432-350	Joel
332	Isaiah XXIV-XXVII
300-200	Zechariah IX-XIV ("II Zech.")
170	I Enoch I-XXXVI (Visions and Journeys)
166	I Enoch LXXXIII-XC (History of Israel)
165	Daniel
140	Sibylline Oracles, Proem and Book III (Greek)
110	I Enoch LXXII-LXXXII (Astronomical Secrets)
109-106	Testaments of the XII Patriarchs
105	Book of Jubilees
104-95	I Enoch XCI-CVIII (Apocalypse of Weeks)

Other Writings

B.C.	
250ff.	Greek translation of O.T. (LXX)
190-170	Tobit
185	Sirach=Ecclesiasticus
168-163	Prayer of Azariah
150	Song of the Three Young Men
150	Judith
150-100	I Baruch (Greek)
	Letter of Jeremiah (= Bar. VI)
150-50	I Esdras (Greek)
132	Translation of Sirach (Greek)
114	Additions to Esther
104-100	I Maccabees
100	Epistle of Aristeas

Date	Work	Date	Work
100 (?)	Joseph and Asenath	100	Jason of Cyrene (abr. in II Macc.)
		100-50	Prayer of Manasseh
		100	Susanna
		100 (?)	Zadokite Fragments
		100 (?)	Dead Sea Manual of Discipline
		100	Bel and the Dragon
94-64 (or later)	I Enoch xxxvii-lxxi (Parables)	65	II Maccabees
		63-40	Psalms of Solomon
		50	III Maccabees
		50	Wisdom of Solomon
31	Sibylline Oracles, Book iii.1-62	A.D. 1-50	IV Maccabees
7 B.C.-A.D. 29	Assumption of Moses	30-50	Writings of Philo
1-50	Martyrdom of Isaiah		
1-50	Secrets of Enoch (II Enoch)		
40	"Little Apocalypse" in Mark xiii	50-62	Paul's Letters
50	II Thessalonians II	68-110	The Gospels
70ff.	II Baruch ("Syriac Baruch")		
80	Sibylline Oracles, Book iv	75-110	Writings of Josephus
90	II Esdras (=IV Ezra) with additions (ch. i-ii, ca. A.D. 150; ch. xv-xvi, ca. A.D. 250)	80	Revision of Shemoneh Esreh
93	Apocalypse of John (Revelation)		
90-100	Apocalypse of Abraham	100 (?)	Books of Adam and Eve
After 100	Sibylline Oracles, Book v	After 100	III Baruch (Greek)
		150 (?)	II Peter
		210	The Mishnah

Jewish, and early Christian religious thought was "eschatological"—with the exception of such unusual writings as
Ecclesiastes and a few passages in the Wisdom literature. In
contrast with the age-old classical or pagan view of time and
history, with its cycles of recurrence—or even without recurrence, with nothing more than endless duration in an unchanging universe—the Hebrew and Jewish conception took
it for granted that eventually the will of God must prevail, and
therefore the evils in the world must come to an end. The
nations which had trampled Israel in the dust would be
punished; the wicked who had triumphed over the righteous
would be brought to the bar of God's judgment; the pristine
stage of innocence and plenty must eventually be restored.
This teleological pattern of thought is taken for granted not
only by the prophets but also by the psalmists, the wise men,
and the scribes. The fitting symbol of the Hebraic or "prophetic" view of history is the arrow flying to its target, not the
late Egyptian and Hellenistic symbol of *Aiōn* (which means
not eternity but endless duration), namely, the hoop snake
with its tail in its mouth, fit figure of endless cyclic repetition.
For the Hebrew, for the Jew, and for the early Christian, the
profoundest of all truths is that God is working out his purposes,
and if one looks deeply enough into the present he can see even
now the signs of God's activity. It was this "eschatological"
framework or pattern of religious thought which was taken for
granted by "apocalyptic", which goes beyond it and produces
(or assumes) a world view and a type of religious belief and
practice quite distinctive and—in Israel—unique. Its main
features one may list as follows.

2. *Apocalyptic* versus *Eschatological*

Apocalyptic is distinguished from prophecy by:

(1) A mood of far greater strain and tension, due to persecution or present peril or uncertainty and pessimism over the
future. Prophecy also is concerned with the future, but its
mood is never so strained and hectic. This is a psychological
criterion, and it even affects literary style.

(2) Apocalyptic represents the complete abandonment of
human means and wisdom, the complete and exclusive reliance

upon a supernatural salvation. Prophecy tended in this direction, but it still required self-help on man's part.

(3) The background of human struggle and of the drama of redemption is cosmic, heavenly, angelic, supernatural, rather than political and historical. For example, the Judgment will be individual, not just the punishment of the oppressing nations.

(4) The list of the *dramatis personae* of the divine theodicy, and of the coming redemption, includes transcendent figures not usually reckoned with in prophecy: the Son of Man, angels, Satan, and others. The properties also include things not usually found in prophecy: the New Jerusalem, the heavenly temple, and so on.

(5) Absolute monotheism is somewhat modified in the direction of polytheism. Other divine personages enter the scene. For example, the Son of Man, at first a symbol but later viewed as a person.

(6) In apocalyptic, more emphasis is placed upon the remoteness and transcendence of God. The naïve and sometimes anthropomorphic idea of God found in the Old Testament and in the oldest rabbinic literature is abandoned, and also the unquestioning attribution to God of personal (that is, human) traits. God is the lofty absolute Ruler of the Universe, predestinating all things. This is perhaps the source of the later, and still popular, idea that Judaism worshipped a "remote" God, separated from contact with the world, and unapproachable by his worshippers except through sacrifice! This was even more true of Philo than of the apocalyptists; but it was not true at all of everyday Jewish piety.

(7) The modes of communication, both divine and human, are supernatural or at least supernormal. Visions, dreams, apparitions, and heavenly voices are far more common than in prophecy—in fact they become the normal mode of communication with the supernatural world. With this may be compared both the primitive beginnings of prophecy, in which these supernormal modes of communication were assumed, and the development of religion in the contemporary Hellenistic world, where the revival of primitive ideas, practices, and presuppositions was also common.

(8) At the same time it is characteristic of apocalyptic that the visions are written down, not related orally: by contrast, the ancient prophet was primarily a speaker, and written prophecy came later than oral. Some of the visions were supposed to be not only written but "sealed" and kept secret until the time of fulfilment drew near. This accounted for the late production—or the presumed discovery—of the visions of certain ancient worthies, such as Adam, Enoch, Noah, Moses, and the fact that they had not hitherto been known and were certainly not included in the recognised scriptures (cf. II Esdras XIV.37-48).

(9) Attention is given to a regimen of spiritual activity. Fasting is practised, not merely as *askēsis* or self-discipline, but as a means to spiritual insight, intuition, power, or authority. A whole apparatus of spiritual controls was set up for achieving the end of clairvoyance and clairaudition.

(10) Apocalyptic prediction of the future is explicit, circumstantial, and unconditional, with no attention paid to human factors, no "if" or "unless". Mark XIII.20 provides a good example: "If the Lord had not shortened the days . . ."; but *already* the days have been shortened, already the plan has been altered, and no further alteration is possible, either as a result of human repentance or as a consequence of the Lord changing his mind (as in the Old Testament). On the other hand, the tone and the formula of prophecy is always, "Unless [or if] you repent . . ." (cf. Luke XIII.3, 5). Prophecy leaves the future open: God is free to act, and possibly men may repent.

(11) For apocalyptic, history unwinds itself toward a final goal, by divine predestination, with no possibility of change or alteration either in direction or in course, not even by the will of God! All the possibilities have already been canvassed, in the divine mind; and what has been decreed and is now taking place is the *right* course, in view (by divine foreknowledge) of all the possibilities and open alternatives in the changing situation. God has foreseen all these, and in the predestined course of events he has already taken them into full account. He is, so to speak, never taken by surprise.

The great pivotal, catastrophic event toward which all history tends is the Day of Judgment. With the prophets, *a* judgment was usually impending, or several successive days of judgment; though the idea of *the* Day of Judgment was probably implicit in Amos' interpretation of "the Day of the Lord" (see p. 70).

(12) Apocalyptic is derived in part from unfulfilled, that is, deferred, prophecy, with an interpretation of the present in the light of its specific details and a prediction of the future in terms of God's purposes which these had indicated. No students of the Bible have ever taken the ancient prophets more seriously or more literally than did the apocalyptists, poring over every detail and fitting them all into a rigid scheme of history! As the rabbis fitted every detail of the Bible into the system of Halakah (religious duty), so the apocalyptists fitted together every tiny detail of eschatological prediction. Both procedures were inevitable in a religion which took divine revelation seriously and literally and identified the revelation with the total contents of a sacred book.

(13) Though the prediction of the future is explicit and unconditional, constant use is made of symbols, sometimes artistically and intricately conceived, sometimes more or less mystical in import, and sometimes wholly surpassing the reach even of the most vivid imagination. It is notorious that the Christian apocalypse, the Revelation of John, cannot be illustrated by artists—at least not satisfactorily (see, for example, even the superb painting by Hans Memling, reproduced in the illustrated edition of the *Revised Standard Version of the New Testament*, 1955). Many of the attempts, from Byzantine to modern times, and especially in the period following the Reformation, have produced little more than grotesques. The reason for the use of symbolism was in part, no doubt, the need for secrecy—some of the apocalypses, including our book of Revelation, were in effect political pamphlets. The symbols themselves, moreover, were sometimes the result of an elaborate and not always consistent cipher (a lamb is a king, a horn is a king, a stampeding goat is a king, Edom is Rome, and so on). Sometimes the cipher was applied to scripture, and this further complicated the situation, for the symbol might not be entirely relevant to the thing symbolised, and the scripture was clearer before it was "interpreted". Sometimes, also, the symbolism seems to have come out of dreams, and these are

often weird and indescribable. The apocalyptists were both
students of scripture (with "keys" of their own, like our mil-
lennialists) and also mystics and visionaries. Moreover, they
worked in a milieu of tradition; the apparatus of their "visions"
was often as commonplace, among their fellow craftsmen, as
the technical lore of any other writers, or as that of artists,
playwrights, poets, or musicians the world over. All this is
very different from the technique of ancient prophecy—though
the prophets likewise used symbols, and some of the latest of
them already begin to anticipate the apocalyptic *genre*.

(14) Past history is easily recognisable, as a rule; the seer
describes events known to him, either in the immediate past or
the surrounding present, by a thinly veiled symbolism—those
familiar with the events and looking upon them more or less
from his point of view would have little difficulty in interpreting
the symbols.[1]   But when the seer's imagination takes flight
into the future and he undertakes to describe coming events—
still symbolically—we are left wondering. Up to a certain
point his symbolism tallies with known history; after this
point it fails to do so; and the reason is not (as a rule) that we
are insufficiently informed of the details of the following period
—the reason is that the events simply did *not* tally, thereafter,
the future did not unroll as the seer had expected. This helps
us to date the writing: the precise point of the take-off in his
flight is the point at which the writer lives. There is little of
this in prophecy. The prophet can usually be dated by his
references to contemporary history, not by the inaccuracy of
his predictions of the future.

(15) Underlying this complicated apocalyptic scheme of
interpretation of the past, the present, and the future is a
profound philosophy of history derived from the Old Testament
prophets. It is a philosophy which takes for granted the
sovereignty of the will of God, not only in human affairs but
also in the vast reaches of the cosmos. Sun, moon, stars, and
earth—all nature, and the deeps beneath—are subject to
God's almighty will and serve his purposes. Hence miracles
and signs are commonplace and everyday: cannot God do

---

[1] For a modern example, see the account of World War II "as an ancient
apocalyptist might have described it", in Ch. VI of my book, *How to Read the Bible*
(New York, Morehouse 1957; Edinburgh, Nelson, 1959).

---

what he will with his own? And although (as we noted above, under § 10) slight changes in schedule are possible, the general system is rigid and predestinarian. Men cannot change the scheme, even by repentance and obedience (as in the prophetic eschatology). Only God can alter it: he may "shorten the days", that is, speed up the process, in order to spare the elect and reduce their sufferings; or he may "lengthen the days", in order to allow the wicked an extension of time in which to repent (cf. p. 68); but in either case the main outlines of the scheme are not changed. The schedule of local stops may be changed a little, so to speak, but the time of the main stops and of the final arrival at destination is not to be altered. Like the schedules of modern railways and armies, the main features were unalterable: history is a complicated web, and cannot be stretched very far one way or another. In the Apocalypse of John, for example, each great act or event leads up to others, to a whole series of new acts and events. But without the antecedent events, the later would be impossible—or very different.

This is true of all human experience, especially of the bitter experience of hope deferred, of the receding goal, of delay in judgment. We all understood the apocalyptic psychology well enough during the war: endurance was possible up to a point, but, as we looked ahead, it seemed utterly impossible beyond that point. Yet the point was reached, and still the end lay far beyond us. We could endure for six months, but no longer; or perhaps for a year; but months lengthened into years, and the years lengthened out to six, before victory came in view. This characteristic, profoundly human "foreshortening of the future", already common in Hebrew prophecy, was also recognisable in apocalyptic: the end will come soon, but—"the end is not yet!"

3. The Permanent Value of Apocalyptic

If anything in the New Testament needs to be "demythologised" it is surely the apocalyptic hope with its traditional imagery, its strange concepts, figures, symbols, presuppositions, its idea of history and even its conception of God. As always in religion and in religious literature, the test is simple: What

does this system of thought—or collection of fancies—do to
the idea of God? If it makes God unworthy of our trust and
confidence, or turns him into an arbitrary tyrant or absolute
monarch "above the law", then the system must be given up.
By this test, quite apart from its failure to predict the later
course of events, apocalyptic is discredited. We can understand it; we can allow for it; we can see why men accepted
it, handed it on, amplified and deepened it, made it—in some
cases—the basis of profound theological views; and, when the
apocalyptic dream finally faded, we can realise how it left
them in the grip of dark cosmic speculations which the church
found it necessary to repudiate and destroy. But behind the
two or three centuries of Jewish and early Christian apocalyptic
enthusiasm and its literature lay the whole long history of
prophetism, with its heroic faith in God, its assurance of the
final triumph of social justice and personal righteousness, its
conviction that the ways of God, though obscure to us, are
wholesome and good and lead in the end to the full realisation
of his purposes. The "truth" in apocalyptic is precisely—and
only—what it shares with prophecy, not the features which
mark it off as distinct and different. Read in this way,
apocalyptic, from the book of Daniel to the Revelation of
John, becomes a vast and weirdly beautiful literature of religious
symbolism, defying both concrete conception and concrete
representation, but full of endless charm and inspiration—for
those who can grasp it. Only, the unwary, the literal-minded,
the prosaic should be sheltered from it, and warned away!

Modern research has shown that there are sharp and very
important differences in origin, in psychology, in religious
authority, and in actual formulation between ancient Hebrew
prophetism and Jewish apocalyptic. To lump the two together,
and describe Jesus as an "apocalyptist" because he spoke of
the coming Kingdom of God; or to ignore the clear marks of
differentiation between the apocalyptic element in the gospels
(or in the New Testament as a whole) and all the rest; or to
use the terms "apocalyptic" and "eschatological" interchangeably—all this leads only to confusion in the interpretation of
the New Testament, and is possible only on the assumption
that Judaism was either unconcerned with the future or

produced only "false" prophets and "false" messiahs (see Mark
XIII and parallels), and had no means of distinguishing seers
and visionaries from the true messengers of God to his people.
Here once more ancient prejudice stands in the way of correct
interpretation, and must be removed before the various
factors in primitive Christianity can be properly weighed and
understood. It truly was an apocalyptic messianic movement;
but deeper than that it was a purely religious movement based
on ancient revelation, a revelation which had now reached its
climax in the life and teaching, death and resurrection of God's
true Servant, Jesus of Nazareth. As we shall see, and as
modern research makes abundantly clear, Jesus was a prophet,
not a wild-eyed dreamer of bizarre and esoteric dreams, or a
devotee of the ascetic routine which led to these secret dis-
closures of the future.

H

Part Three

THE NEW TESTAMENT

CHAPTER SEVEN

Jesus the Galilean

Jesus was a Galilean. The fact scarcely needs to be stated, yet its significance is often overlooked. Even the advocates of the foolish "Aryan" theory, thirty years ago, though they denied that Jesus was a Jew nevertheless acknowledged that he was born and reared in Galilee. (This strange theory formed a part of the lunatic dream of Nazi racial superiority; it was based on the antiquated anthropology of Max Müller and that of the nineteenth century "Nordic" enthusiasts.) The "Jewishness" of Jesus should never have been questioned. The reasons for doing so are obviously derived from "anti-Semitic" prejudice. The New Testament everywhere takes it for granted that Jesus was both a Jew and a Galilean, so much so that the problem of his origin in that northern district stands in the way of Jewish recognition of his prophetic call (see John VII.52). The stories told in the Infancy Narratives of Luke and Matthew are designed to show how it came about that a *Galilean* could fulfill the ancient prophecy that the Messiah was to be born in Bethlehem of Judea.

But it is not these historical details which concern us at present; it is the broader significance of the great fact that Jesus' homeland was Jewish, Palestinian, Galilean. The importance of this fact is one of the presuppositions of all modern study of the life of Jesus, beginning with Ernest Renan's famous *Vie de Jésus* in 1863, and more fully recognised in such essays as those by Walter Bauer and Walther Sattler in the *Festgabe* published in honour of Adolf Jülicher in 1927. It is also recognised in many other modern works, both popular and scholarly. The recent book by Sherman E. Johnson,

Jesus in His Homeland (1957),[1] takes the fact and its significance entirely for granted and proceeds to draw out the further inferences and implications. Not in the priestly atmosphere of Jerusalem, not in some semi-barbarous nomadic tent-village on the edge of the great eastern desert, not among the half-heathen outcast Samaritans, not in a Hellenistic town like those in the Decapolis, not among the wandering shepherds on the dry barren upland of the South Country, but in populous, busy, highly civilised and also deeply religious Galilee, among devout and earnest observant Jews—this is where Jesus grew to manhood. This is where, humanly speaking (how can we speak otherwise?), his whole outlook on life was shaped and matured. Perhaps the best way to begin a study of ancient Judaism is to look at that religion as Jesus saw it, day by day, in his home town, his *patris* or "father-city" (as Mark calls it, VI.1), where he was "accustomed" (Luke IV.16) to attend the synagogue.

1. *Social Conditions in Galilee*

Here Jesus' family lived—at Nazareth, a hill town in Lower Galilee overlooking the fertile, populous Plain of Esdraelon. There were two good reasons, in ancient times, for building a city "on a hill" (Matt. v.14); one was for health—people then thought, as in Italy they still think, that the verdant lowlands cause fevers; the other was for safety—though Nazareth, unlike many other hill towns, had no surrounding stone wall. The chief problem was the water supply; but as in the legendary yet typical town of Bethulia, scene of the thrilling heroic tale of the Book of Judith (VI.11), springs bubbled up at the foot of the hill, and it was not too distant or toilsome a journey to carry up the water, a jar at a time. This was women's work, in the East, and it afforded each day an opportunity for a social gathering at the fountain. Here the younger women and girls gathered, with their water jars carried on their heads, and chatted for a while with their neighbours before trudging back up the hill to their homes. Here each day Mary, accompanied by the boy Jesus, and also by the younger children in the family (Mark VI.3) as they

---

[1] English edition, *Jesus in His Own Times* (London, Black, 1958).

grew big enough for the walk, would come for water. The place is still called the Virgin's Fountain, by both Christians and Muslims, in memory of Jesus' mother.

The industries of the town were simple. Some persons tilled the surrounding hillsides, sowing their fields with barley and harvesting it in what would seem to us early spring; others trimmed vines, tended the growing grapes, and gathered them for the autumn vintage; others worked in the orchards, and nursed the figs, the olives, and the apples, or the melons that grew on the ground among the trees; others engaged in trade, or made articles for household or personal use—shoes and sandals, donkey saddles, lamps, lampstands, or mantles and tunics and turbans, or the heavier woven cloth used for bedding or tents. The little workshops were located inside the simple one-room houses of their owners, even as they are today in the eastern Mediterranean world, from Sicily to Syria, Palestine, and Egypt.

Among them, one household was centred in the building trade. Joseph was a "carpenter", as we translate the word; but as the term was used then it meant a builder—*tektōn*, that is, literally, and originally, a roofer. He made wooden ploughs, window-frames, chairs and tables, but he also built houses with doors and roofs. Most of these houses were very simple, with walls of tamped earth or sun-dried brick; only rarely was a peasant house built of stone. Over such simple dwellings the roof was laid with saplings and branches upon which moist clay was patted down and left to bake in the sun. Many families would of course build their own houses, make their own furniture and implements. The better houses, though uncommon except in the hill country, were built of stone, and required the work of skilled masons; as a "builder" Joseph may also have been a mason. The trades were then not as sharply distinguished as they are today. Timber was very scarce. Palestine had originally been a well-forested land, but by the first century the timber had been cut down, and the arid treeless aspect of the country was already what it has been ever since—though the Israelis are now planting thousands of trees, and may succeed in bringing back the land to its former state, well watered, fruitful, and vastly more productive than it has been for the past 1800 years.

There was work enough for all, in the Galilee of those days. The words of the man in Jesus' parable, "I cannot dig; to beg I am ashamed" (Luke XVI.3), were only the lame excuse of a rascal. All Palestine, in those days, was crowded but far from prosperous. The old system still prevailed, with private ownership, patriarchal customs, primitive agriculture and grazing, family co-operation in toil. The spreading prosperity of the Roman world had not yet reached Palestine; it never did reach Palestine, in fact, for two terrible wars, and the constant social and political unrest which preceded and followed them, with repeated outbreaks of violence, effectively prevented it.[1] There were many beggars; yet the man who was willing to work found plenty to do. Some scholars imagine that Joseph found further employment in the rebuilding of Sepphoris, up in the hills to the north-west, four miles from Nazareth. This city had been destroyed by the Romans in A.D. 6 but was now being rebuilt by Herod Antipas to serve as his temporary capital while he finished building Tiberias on the lake of Galilee. The new city was to be Roman in style, with a theatre and an aqueduct—these involved masonry, and so did the Roman style of houses; and here was located Antipas's treasury, until the outbreak of the war against Rome in the year 66. It was designed to be one of the finest of modern cities, in its time.

2. *"Galilee of the Gentiles"*

Galilee had not always been Jewish. Its very name was *Galil hagoyim*, the "circle of the Gentiles", either because it was a territory surrounded by foreign peoples or because it contained settlements of Jews surrounded by Gentile neighbours. In the first century many non-Jews lived there, especially Syrians, Phoenicians, Arameans, Greeks, and Romans. Some of these foreigners were descendants of the peoples who crowded into northern Palestine after the fall of Samaria (in 722 B.C.) or during the period of the Exile (the century or

---

[1] On the economic condition of Palestine during the lifetime of Jesus, see my *Economic Background of the Gospels* (Oxford, 1926), and the essay on "The Economic Background of the New Testament", in *The Background of the New Testament and its Eschatology*, ed. by W. D. Davies and D. Daube (Cambridge, 1956), with the bibliography, pp. 99ff.

more following 597 B.C.), or during the terrible days of the
Maccabean War (which began in 168 B.C.), when the whole
Jewish population of Galilee had been evacuated for safety to
Judea.   Some were descendants of the veterans of Alexander
the Great and his successors, especially of the Seleucid kings, who
had been given land and special privileges, such as exemption
from taxation, and lived in the Decapolis or "Ten Towns"
nearby.   Even though these foreigners had lived in Galilee for
several generations, they were still looked upon as strangers,
goyim (foreigners) or *gērim* (resident aliens); for the Holy
Land belonged to Israel, by God's special grant or lease, and
others were admitted only on sufferance, and were not really
welcome unless they became full-fledged Jews in faith and
practice, that is, proselytes to Judaism.   Many of them did
become Jews, during the first century before Christ and the
first century after, and they came from all over the world.
Those who decided to settle permanently in Palestine added
greatly to its problems of over-population and food supply.
And so it was that Galilee was not entirely Jewish, even in the
first century.

From the hilltop of Nazareth, Jesus could catch a glimpse
of the far-away lands to the north, the east and the south, and
to the distant Mediterranean Sea in the west.   Here he could
see the dark ships with their white sails, plying their coastwise
journeys from Egypt to Asia Minor and the west.   For in
ancient times, before the compass was invented, ships usually
followed the coast.   Moreover, for much of the season open to
navigation each year, the prevailing winds were from the
north and north-west, and this often made sailing directly
westward impossible.   Far to the north rose majestic snow-
capped Mount Hermon, standing like a silent angel on guard
over God's people, though it was now surrounded, even as
they were, by the pagans.   There was even a new pagan city
at the foot of the mountain.   Like Sepphoris and Tiberias it
also had been built by one of the sons of Herod the Great—by
Philip, the tetrarch of north-eastern Palestine.   He had named
it Caesarea, in honour of the Roman emperor Augustus,
and it was commonly known as Caesarea Philippi, "Philip's
Caesarea", to distinguish it from another Caesarea on the
Mediterranean coast a few miles south of Mount Carmel.   Off

to the east lay the distant hills and the high tableland of eastern Galilee, where now there were still more pagan cities, especially beautiful Gerasa, built of shining marble, with temples and theatre and market place, all very unlike the traditional Jewish architecture of cities. They also differed greatly in social customs and in religious beliefs and practices from Jewish towns like Nazareth.

To the south-east lay the wide canyon of the river Jordan, the "Descender", as it dropped down ever deeper in its gorge and finally flowed into the Dead Sea at 1286 feet (almost a quarter-mile) below sea-level. From this sea there was no outlet, and so the waters evaporated in the blazing hot sunshine and gave it another name, the "Salt Sea". Near the mouth of the Jordan, where it entered the northern end of the Dead Sea, there was a settlement of Jewish monks, perhaps members of the Essene order; the remains of their library, stored away for safety in sealed jars, have recently (1947) been recovered from the nearby caves of Qumrân, and are now being studied by scholars the world over—the so-called "Dead Sea Scrolls". More directly to the south rose the mountains of Samaria, long known as the "watchtower" or "outpost" (Shōmrōn) guarding the passes on the northern borders of Judea. But Samaria was now another half-Gentile region; its people were descendants of the "five nations" which the Assyrian conquerors had transplanted there after the destruction of Samaria in 722 B.C. Once it had been the luxurious capital of the Northern Kingdom of Israel; but now it was a miserable shadow of its former self, even though the Romans had undertaken to restore it, and had given it the name Sebastē (or, in Latin, Augusta), likewise in honour of the emperor. The Samaritans had a version of the Pentateuch in their own language (Samaritan) as their only Bible, and by its guidance they tried to observe the religion of the country; but they were scorned and detested by the orthodox Jews of Jerusalem and Judea. They were described as "that feeble folk which dwells in Shechem", for the Jews had "no dealings with the Samaritans", since salvation was "from the Jews" (Sirach L.26, John IV.9, 22).

Thus it was mainly a pagan world that surrounded the boy Jesus as he looked off into the distance from his hilltop

home in Nazareth—pagan, and bitter with enmity and prejudice, paralysed by racial and religious taboos, and waiting
for some healing word of reconciliation and peace and an
ordered way of life under the coming Reign of God. At his
feet lay still another reminder of the "ways of the Gentiles"
and of the vast distances that separated the East from the West.
It was the ancient highway which came up along the coast
from Egypt, crossed over through the pass at ancient Megiddo,
wended its peaceful way across the Plain of Esdraelon, and
then wound up and over and down the other side of the nearby
eastern hills to Capernaum, the thriving town on the northern
shore of the Lake of Galilee. Capernaum was out of sight of
Nazareth, for it lay down in the valley, 680 feet below sea-
level. Here custom duties were collected on goods passing
through or into the country—some duties were collected even
on goods exported from the country! Then on went the
ancient road, northward and eastward to Damascus, to Pal-
myra, to Babylon, to far-away India and China.

3. *Political Conditions in Palestine*

Not only was his homeland surrounded by Gentiles, but
the whole country of Palestine was in process of absorption by
the Romans. Their forces of occupation were everywhere. The
local rulers in Galilee and the north-east, the surviving sons of
Herod, paid tribute in order to keep their thrones as tetrarchs,
and were required to manifest their good will and their good
faith by many acts of friendliness and even of subservience.
Judea and Samaria, in the south, were already ruled by Roman
governors, "procurators", whose business it was to collect taxes,
maintain peace and order, and induce the Jewish people to
accept the new regime. For Rome's policies were determined
by the general situation throughout the Near East. Two long
centuries of war and revolution in the West, beginning with
the Second Punic War, had disturbed the peace of the entire
world. The Parthians still roamed the eastern deserts, and
once at least had invaded Palestine on their swift horses,
clouding the sky with their arrows, and leaving death and
destruction behind them. There was of course no natural
frontier against the desert, or anywhere in fact from the Black
Sea to the Red. Therefore the Romans undertook to construct

a "living wall' of subject but satisfied peoples, all the length of this vast distance—over eight hundred miles. In the north they were not very successful: Armenia never really submitted. In the centre they succeeded magnificently: Syria became one of the most completely Romanised provinces in the empire. In the south they failed, and the Jews, after the two awful wars of A.D. 66-70 and A.D. 132-135, with possibly still another revolt in the days of Trajan, were doomed to be crushed and scattered.

The political situation in Jesus' lifetime was the preliminary stage of growing tension, distrust, and animosity which led to the tragic events of the sixties. Even then, in Jesus' boyhood, there were camps of "Zealots" (that is, those zealous for the sacred Law, with a slogan, "No king but God") in the hills of Galilee, where they combined robbery with patriotism and hid their loot in caves. Here Herod the Great, when a young officer in search of distinction, had burned them out by lowering himself with a few men over the cliffs and then tossing fiery brands inside the caves. Thus it was no happy, contented world, the one in which Jesus was born and grew to manhood. Instead, it had all those features of torment and oppression, of racial antagonism, violence, bigotry and fanaticism, totalitarianism and genocide, which have maimed and marred our own days.

And yet the hope of better things still glowed in human hearts, not only among the Jews but also among the pagans. The emperor Augustus, under whom Jesus was born, had dedicated himself to the establishment of peace on earth, after crushing the enemies of his country and the coalition which had undertaken to wrest Egypt and the East from Roman control. That dangerous scheme had been the plot of Antony and Cleopatra; but the future emperor had defeated them at Actium in 31 B.C., and from then onward his policy was peace with justice, and the "restoration of the Republic". The results were encouraging, and prosperity followed close on universal peace—wherever peace was allowed to prevail. In the Province of Asia, for example, in western Asia Minor, Augustus was hailed as the Saviour of men, the bringer of world peace, in language resembling the Song of the Angels in Luke II.14, and his birthday was made the New Year's Day for the whole province. Earlier still the poet Virgil, in his beautiful *Fourth Eclogue*, had described the idyllic conditions about to prevail.[1] Many scholars think the Roman poet may have read the Old Testament book of the prophet Isaiah in the Greek translation.

4. *The Hope for Better Days to Come*

Among the Jews, the ancient hope of a Messiah, the "Anointed" who was to be chosen, appointed, and sent by God himself, flamed up once more in ever brighter hues. Some thought he would be an earthly king, reigning with a magnificence of luxury and power equal to the glorious days of the earlier "Son of David", King Solomon—whose empire had reached from sea to sea (Ps. LXXII.8), that is, from the Dead Sea to the Mediterranean, and from the mountains of the north to the rivers of the south, that is, to the Gulf of Akabah and the border of Egypt. Others—as we have seen— thought he would be a purely supernatural figure, coming on the clouds of heaven, as the "Son of Man" or the "Primal Man" or the "Man from Heaven", and would judge the whole world, its kings and potentates, both men and angels, and even demons. Then, after the Last Judgment, he would usher in a purely heavenly, transcendental, spiritual state of things which should last for ever and ever.

The beautiful hymns which are found in the first two chapters of Luke's gospel set forth the first of these two views; here the political dream is shot through with inspired religious feeling and insight. If these hymns reflect the spirit of Jesus' home in Nazareth; if his people were these same humble, devoted, consecrated Jewish pietists, the "pious and humble in the land"; if the deep religious feeling which throbs in these glorious poems was also the feeling which dominated his home in Nazareth; if the spirit of that home was—as is almost always the case in religious homes—the creation of his blessed mother; if this was the spirit of religious devotion in which Jesus lived and breathed, and which he absorbed from his infancy—the noblest ancient Jewish piety, identical with the devotion of the Psalms and the prophets, especially Isaiah and

[1] See my *Ancient Roman Religion* (New York, Liberal Arts Press, 1957), pp. 185ff.

Jeremiah: then, if our premise is correct, it was perfectly natural and all but inevitable that Jesus, so far as we can describe him in psychological terms, should become the person he was. Or, put in another way, the most natural and inevitable surroundings of the Divine One whom God himself had sent to his people and to all mankind, were those of this humble, beautiful, consecrated Jewish home. For there was no religious piety in the whole ancient world to equal that of the Jewish home, no religion to match Judaism in its devotion and earnestness, its self-abnegation and loyalty. Alas that it could also be misled and misused by unscrupulous, ambitious, fanatical leaders!

5. *The Birth of the Messiah*

Everyone knows the Christmas story—its fullest record is in Luke, chapters I and II. But how are we to interpret it? The popular modern view of history is, of course, very literal. Either an event must have happened exactly as it is described, or it happened not at all—and the record must be discarded as false. We have a prejudice in favour of literalism; our standard of historical accuracy is the court reporter's record—or preferably, now, the electronic tape. But this standard cannot be applied to ancient literature, including the Bible. As a matter of fact, ancient literature contains very few stories of the birth and infancy of great men, and certainly nothing like the deeply religious narrative of Luke with its idyllic mingling of past, present, and future, its glowing messianism, its all-pervading celestial overtones of inspired human utterance and angelic song. The central story is the Annunciation, the angel's message to Mary predicting the birth of her son, who is to be "great, and will be called the Son of the Most High"; to him will be given

> the throne of his father David,
> And he will reign over the house of Jacob for ever;
> And of his kingdom there will be no end. (Luke 1.32f.)

Of course, this prophecy uses the language of the ancient hope of a Messiah—the glorious supernatural king who should sit on David's throne, free the nation, and establish a purely religious, theocratic Utopia which would last for ever, thus taking the place of all other earthly thrones and powers—the Roman, and all others. This hope has never been fulfilled, save in the "spiritual" sense, as Christ reigns in human hearts and so gradually brings peace to the world.

Some of the Renaissance artists pictured the scene most appropriately: as the angel approaches, the Blessed Virgin is seen kneeling in prayer or meditation, or reading from the Bible. Had we asked them, "What part of the Bible?" they would have replied, "One chapter, of course!" This was the seventh chapter of Isaiah, where it is said (v. 14), "The Lord himself will give you a sign: Behold, a young woman [the Greek version reads, 'a virgin'] shall conceive and bear a son, and shall call his name Immanuel" (that is, "God with us"). In place of the terrible dangers and deprivations of Isaiah's time, there was hope that God himself would soon turn darkness into light, mourning into joy, and that a baby born in this new day would have a divinely chosen name, "God *with* us", not against us![1] And if this promise had been true and valid in Isaiah's time, over seven hundred years before, in spite of all the dangers from Damascus and other hostile powers, might it not be true even now, in spite of the hostile power of Rome and all other enemies that threatened to annihilate God's people and their religion, the sacred Covenant and the sacred Law?

Two of the old Italian painters, Leonardo da Vinci and Antonello da Messina, thus represented Mary looking into the book open before her, and so did Jan van Eyck in the surviving fragment from the lost triptych of Dijon. Many persons believe this idea to be sound and true. For behind Jesus, his mission and his message, was the life of the family in which he was reared; and at the centre of this family was his consecrated mother; and behind her years of piety and devotion lay that hour of sudden inspiration and revelation; and behind that hour was the noble character of her earlier years— divine revelation never comes to the unworthy. In the exalted assurance that she was to bear a child, a son, she dreamed of what he might be: her people's saviour, redeemer, and king. No doubt she too, like everyone else, thought of the Messiah

[1] Or, more literally, "With us is God!" Compare Paul's affirmation in Rom. VIII.31-39. An alternative chapter would be Isa. IX.

as an earthly ruler, though possessing supernatural qualities, even as Isaiah, long before, had described him (see Isa. IX.1-7). But, as always, under God's divine over-ruling, the prophecy was destined to be not only fulfilled but over-fulfilled, with new and profounder meanings, and with farther-reaching consequences than anyone could realise at the time. It was to be fulfilled, even when it was *not* fulfilled; it was to be fulfilled, and *over*-fulfilled, even though it was also to be frustrated and denied, in its literal sense. For this Son of God, like his own people, and also like his own closest followers down the centuries, was destined to achieve no easy victory. His own call, and his calling, was not only to live but to die—in order to live and to bring life to others.

For many readers, the Infancy Narrative in Luke is centred in the miracle of the Virgin Birth. But the Virgin Birth is really incidental, and could even be omitted—even then the story would hold together with perfect unity and continuity. Perhaps the story was originally told by Luke—or by those before Luke—without reference to the miracle. At least, there are now many scholars who thus interpret Luke's opening chapters.[1] The idea of the Virgin Birth really belongs to Matthew, where it is integral and indispensable to the narrative, and where it is introduced as a Jewish-Christian explanation (what in Jewish literature is called a *midrash*) of the Greek translation—*not* the Hebrew original—of the passage in Isaiah VII.14. The translation of Luke 1.34 in some modern versions is quite wrong and betrays the influence of modern exegesis and theology, which stress the impossibility of the miracle from a naturalistic or scientific standpoint. The Greek text really agrees with the old King James or "Authorised" Version and the nineteenth century Revised: it is not "How *can* this be?"

---

[1] The words in 1.34, "Seeing I know not a man" (AV) or "Since I have no husband" (RSV)—only four words in Greek—must be a gloss, like the one in III.23 ("as was supposed"). The words are inconsistent with the presuppositions of the Lucan narrative: Mary is betrothed to Joseph, and will undoubtedly be married to him before long. Indeed the reader already knows that Jesus was the son of Mary. For ancient Judaism, betrothal was virtually equivalent to marriage, and lacked only the act of consummation and the living together of the husband and wife. Like a marriage, a betrothal could be ended only by death or divorce. It was much more serious than a modern engagement or "understanding". See my art., " Where Form Criticism and Textual Criticism Overlap", in the *Journal of Biblical Literature*, LIX, 11-21.

but "How *shall* this be?" Unlike Zacharias (Luke 1.18, 45),
Mary does not doubt the angel's words, but is mystified over
the destiny of her son-to-be: *How* shall he become "great, . . .
the Son of the Most High", a king seated on the throne of
David—his ancestor, 1.27—ruling a kingdom which shall never
end? She does not ask the superfluous question, "How *can*
this be?" that is, how is she to have a son? Is she not betrothed
and about to be married? Is it not the dearest dream of her
heart, as it is the dream of every Jewish bride, that she shall
have a son? In reality the question is one more of Luke's
characteristic leading questions, which all but answer themselves, and are based on what he is about to introduce into his
narrative: questions like "Will those who are saved be few?"—
of course! (XIII.23); or "Are you telling this parable for us or
for all?"—certainly for all (XII.41); or "Will you at this time
restore the kingdom to Israel?"—of course not! (Acts 1.6). It
is quite characteristic of Luke's superb literary style to introduce sayings and incidents in this way. (See also Luke
XVIII.41, Acts XIX.2f.; there are many examples.) In good
literature, when dialogue is used, such leading questions are
often employed: they are designed to introduce or to lead up
to the correct answer, or even to suggest it. Here the question
concerns the way in which her son is to achieve his quasi-
supernatural destiny, *not* the biological possibility of his birth;
and the answer is appropriate and convincing: he will achieve
his divine destiny as a consequence of the overshadowing of
the Holy Spirit, from the instant of his conception; moreover,
the presence and the power of the Holy Spirit will overshadow
not only the child but his mother (1.35). If anyone wishes to
see an example of a *biological* question, let him turn to the story
of Nicodemus in John III.4, "How *can* a man be born when he
is old?"—the Greek is as clear as the English, and both imply
the utter impossibility of such a thing. See also VI.52—where
the same language is used. Simply as a matter of style, if *Luke*
had said, "How *can* this be?" the question would certainly
have implied impossibility; and that would have been totally
out of character, on Mary's lips.

The rest of the story is consistent with this interpretation.
Luke 1.38 expresses Mary's eager acceptance of her role, as
Mother of the Messiah—not her willingness to bear a child,

I

or to bear a child without a human father. The phrase "to me" parallels the "of you" in v. 35. Verses 41-45 are equally a celebration of the coming Messiah, not a recognition that Mary is pregnant. Verse 56, which attaches to v. 36, implies that Mary *left* Elizabeth at the end of her period of pregnancy but before the birth of her child (in the ancient world the period was often reckoned as *ten* months)—which is strange, and suggests editorial manipulation. Verse 57, "son", is in fulfilment of 1.13. Luke 11.5 reads "wife" in many manuscripts, or "betrothed wife" (which is merely a textual conflation, designed to correct or improve the term "wife"). The poetry in 11.14, 29ff., 34f., is all in celebration of the birth of the *Messiah*, with no reference to the Virgin Birth.

The basic biblical passage in support of the doctrine of the Virgin Birth is not Luke 1.26-38 or Gal. iv.4 or Rev. xii.5 or the Old Latin variant in John 1.13, but Matt. 1.18-25, which begins, "Now the birth of the Christ [or the Messiah; see Vulgate and RSV mg.] took place in this way . . ." This clear, comprehensive, categorical statement could not be more explicit. But *in its form* it is really a "midrash" upon Isaiah vii.14, not in the original Hebrew but in the Greek translation.

In place of the usual interpretation which most of us, being literalists, have forced upon this ancient story, its true significance, I believe, is that it makes the character of Jesus' mother stand out—as Luke meant it to stand out—full of meaning for the whole life of Jesus, his character, his destiny, and his triumph. In a time when civilisation itself is gravely threatened, when family life everywhere is in jeopardy, the character and the example of this simple, devout, saintly Jewish woman, the mother of Jesus, and of the home which she created, may turn out to be almost the greatest legacy of ancient Judaism to the Christian church, and, more than that, to all mankind. No religion in the ancient world gave a higher place to women. In her own home, the Jewish wife and mother was a priestess, with privileges no one could share. She alone lighted the Sabbath lamp on Friday evening, with a brief meditation and a prayer which in its present form is among the most beautiful in the Jewish Prayer Book.

Father of mercy, continue thy loving-kindness to me and to my dear ones. Make me worthy to rear my children so that they will walk in the way of the righteous before thee, loyal to thy Law and continually engaged in good deeds. Keep far from us all manner of shame, grief, and care; and grant that peace, light, and joy may ever abide in our home. For with thee is the fountain of light, and in thy light we see light. *Amen.*

The form of the prayer is medieval, but its spirit is ancient. The custom of saying it was observed in the second century, and earlier (see Mishnah, *Shabbath* II.6).

6. *The Church in Galilee*

Galilee was important as the background of Jesus' early life and ministry; it was also important for the history of the early church. Fifty years ago, the question was often debated whether or not there was ever any early Christian church in Galilee. The gospels and Acts are markedly silent on the subject—with the consequence that the few indications which survive, pointing toward the existence of a Galilean church, are all the more significant. The woes on the Galilean cities (Luke x.13-15, Matt. xi.20-24) do not include all of Galilee; the references in Acts (xxi.3, 16) to disciples in Tyre and to an "early disciple" somewhere between Caesarea and Jerusalem, and to the mission of the apostles in "all Judea and Samaria" (i.8) provide clear evidence that Christians—or "Nazarenes", their earliest name, according to Epiphanius—were to be found in the North and, presumably, in Jesus' own homeland. The absence of any mention of Galilee in Acts i.8 may really presuppose that this territory was already evangelised—by the Lord himself, the Twelve, and the Seventy: Acts ix.31 contains an explicit reference to the church in Galilee. It is in the light of this situation that the command in Mark xvi.7 (cf. xiv.28) must be understood. Not only had Galilee been already evangelised (Matt. iv.12-25), but it was—at the time of the Resurrection—a strong centre, perhaps the strongest centre, of Jesus' followers. The idea that Jesus' own mission in Galilee was a total failure, that he himself at last abandoned it and withdrew to foreign territory, and then returned only to pass through the land incognito on his way to Jerusalem to die, and that there never was a strong Christian movement in northern Palestine, is contrary to all probability as well as to all the (admittedly slight) evidence.

The explanation of the one-sided evidence in the gospels and Acts is clearly (*a*) the theory of Luke, who assumed that Christianity began at Jerusalem and from there spread out into all the world, eventually reaching Rome and evangelising the North-Mediterranean tier of provinces on its way thither. This theory is supported by another, found elsewhere in the New Testament, especially in the Gospel of John, viz. (*b*) that Jesus' "ministry" among his own people was a failure, that he was formally "rejected" by the Jews, and that in consequence the Jews were "rejected" by God—at least temporarily. Whatever we may say of the second theory, that of Luke is an impressive one. It resembles the theories of other ancient historians who wrote with apologetic aims and viewed their task as far more literary than scientific in nature. All ancient historical writing tended more and more, during the rise and spread of Hellenism, and following the triumph of rhetoric in the Greek and Roman schools, to become a branch of literature and to make either persuasive or artistic effectiveness its chief goal. "Luke the historian"—who is of course our only historian for the earliest stage of the Christian religion—was as much influenced by this ideal as anyone else at the time. His apologetic purposes have been clearly demonstrated by modern studies of Luke-Acts, for example those by Henry Cadbury, Burton Scott Easton, J. M. Creed, F. J. Foakes-Jackson, Kirsopp Lake, Ernst Haenchen—to mention some of the best known writers. It was a consequence of Luke's theory that only such cities or countries as Jerusalem, Judea, Samaria, Syria, Anatolia, Macedonia, Greece, and Italy were mentioned: all the rest were neglected. But obviously the gospel had spread in other directions as well. There were Christians, at an early date, in Damascus (Acts ix.10, 19), in the cities of the Coastal Plain (viii.40, ix.32-xi.18), in Ethiopia (viii.26-38), and by implication (Acts ii.9-11, the story of Pentecost) in other equally remote lands. The legends and traditions of the later church confirm this early and sudden expansion of the Christian faith to many far-distant regions.

The theory that Galilee was not a Christian centre from "the first days of the gospel", but required to be re-evangelised by the apostles, is not now so commonly held as it was two generations ago. The position of Johannes Weiss, set forth in his *Primitive Christianity* (English translation, 1937), was based almost exclusively on Luke-Acts. Francis Burkitt held a similar view (see his *Christian Beginnings*, 1924). Professor Benjamin Bacon held a mediating position—Peter's vision of the Lord, when he asked, *Quo vadis, Domine?* was seen not near Rome but near Jerusalem, on his homeward flight to Galilee; he turned about and returned to the city, and there the Christian church was born. But the fullest reversal of the earlier theory came in Ernst Lohmeyer's *Galiläa und Jerusalem* (1937). Here Galilee becomes the holy land of the new revelation, the *terra sancta Christiana*, where the disciples not only saw the Lord, risen and glorified (as in Mark, Matthew, and John XXI), but also were destined to witness his final Parousia, the beginning of the Last Judgment.[1] On this view, Galilee, far from being an abandoned *cul de sac* in the world-wide spread of the gospel, was its centre of radiation, eclipsed by Jerusalem only after the apostles had shifted their headquarters to the nation's capital. This is perhaps an extreme view—the opposite extreme, compared with the one which it displaced. But clearly there is evidence on both sides. And if it is not impossible, either historically, psychologically, or theologically, for the Risen Christ to manifest himself in more than one place, either simultaneously or successively, and if the fragmentary data for a reconstruction of the course of events following the Resurrection point to a number of localities, then surely it is appropriate to follow probability and assume that the Christian church has existed in Galilee from the beginning. The "beginning of the gospel", as Acts x.37f. explicitly states, was in Galilee, "after the baptism which John preached"; for "God anointed Jesus of Nazareth with the Holy Spirit and with power", so that "he went about doing good and healing all that were oppressed by the devil, for God was with him". The movement thus inaugurated was certainly far more successful than the gospels and Acts explicitly state, though they often suggest or imply much more than they tell.[2] The theory of Maurice Goguel and others, viz. that the whole

---

[1] I have summarised Lohmeyer's theory in *The Earliest Gospel* (New York, 1943), Ch. VI.

[2] This is one thesis of my book, *The Gospel of the Kingdom* (New York, 1940).

"Galilean ministry" was a total, tragic failure, so that Jesus'
very enemies warned him to flee for his life (Luke XIII.31),
while his own family thought him unbalanced and tried to
take him home with them (Mark III.21, 31),[1] and his disciples
"drew back and no longer went about with him" (John VI.66)—
this theory goes much too far. Its ultimate absurdity becomes
apparent in Albert Schweitzer's formulation: Jesus in desperation determined to force the hand of God, and in doing so
risked his life—and lost it.

Surely a sounder view will be one more consonant with the
religious ethos and psychology of Judaism and the Old Testament. The prophet may be rejected by many; yet there are
always some thousands "who have not bowed the knee to
Baal" (1 Kings XIX.18), but have remained faithful to God
and loyal to their leader. The seed of the gospel may fall on
different kinds of soil—some barren, some rocky, some weedy,
some thin; yet enough seed falls upon "good ground" to
guarantee the harvest. And though the tales of prophets and
of saints all over the ancient Near East, from Elijah the
Tishbite to Mani the Persian, assure us that religious faith
often thrives under persecution and rises victorious out of
defeat, the terms and conditions must not be totally adverse
and negative; there have been prophets who left behind them
nothing but a name, and some whose very name was forgotten.

The church in Galilee presumably faced harsher vicissitudes
than those confronting other churches. Galilee was more
open to the rising tide of Syrian, Phoenician, and Anatolian
paganism than any other part of Palestine. It lay directly
in the path of the advancing Roman forces in A.D. 66, and
became the battleground of the opening years of the Jewish
war. With the fall of Galilee, Samaria and Judea were open
to Vespasian's legions; thereafter Galilee remained occupied
territory. When the second revolt began, in A.D. 132, the
Christians were compelled by their fellow Jews to serve in the
revolutionary forces mustered by Bar Kozeba—those who
refused were tortured or put to death, much as Christians
have been forcibly drafted into war service in various parts of

[1] I.e., if these two verses refer to the same group, one verse supplying the
motive for the action described in the other—as in H. D. A. Major's strange
reference to "the madness of Jesus" (in *The Mission and Message of Jesus*, 1938).

the world since 1914. And yet the church in Galilee survived, and has survived to this day. I once entertained a Galilean Christian who showed me a small pectoral cross in his possession; it had belonged, he told me, to one of his ancestors, a bishop in Galilee in the fourth century. When I asked how long his family had been Christian, he replied, in astonishment, "From the beginning! We were among the earliest followers of Jesus!" I see no reason to question this claim, or to challenge his pride in such a heritage. As the research of scholars continues, and we come to learn more about the characteristic traits of both Galilean Judaism and Galilean Christianity, I am sure we shall find ourselves somewhat closer to a true understanding of the mind of Christ, his life and character, his teaching, and the "way of God" which he set forth "in truth", both by precept and example.

Modern research in the area of the political, social, and religious background of the life of Jesus, and especially his home life in Nazareth, as far as this can be made out, shows that it included the deep, non-professional piety of the devout Jewish laity. Certainly Jesus was a complete and thorough Jew. The "Nordic" nonsense popular in Germany in the 1930's, with its purely "Aryan" Christ, was utterly impossible. He was no Greek philosopher in disguise, no Indian guru, saint, or ascetic. The thorough "Jewishness" of Jesus is assumed by all present-day scholars competent to judge. But we shall never grasp the full significance of this fact until we abandon the apologetic—but really polemical—approach to the life of Jesus, including the view that he was "rejected" by the Jewish people as a whole, and begin to view his Judaism as something of great positive value, not a weakness, a liability, or a limitation to be denied or explained away. One sometimes wonders how it has been possible for Christians ever to reach the conclusion that Jesus' Jewish nature and inheritance were a liability—until one recalls the intense hatred and bigotry which for long centuries have scorned everything in Judaism as false, hypocritical, and valueless. The consequences of this bigotry and hatred, for the hapless victims, have been tragic enough; but the consequences for Christians, in the interpretation of their own sacred books, have also been disastrous.

CHAPTER EIGHT

The Gospel of
the Kingdom of God

We are often troubled by the fact that we know very little about the life of Jesus or the precise details of his teaching. The average person—the "man in the street" and even the "man in the pew"—assumes that we know much more than we really do, or that careful research would bring out far more information than is now available. This illusion was fostered by the old-fashioned "Lives of Christ" in two or three volumes; but their contents were chiefly discussion of the sources or descriptions of the world in which he lived. The expectation of a detailed life of Jesus is mistaken, and results from demanding of the New Testament the standards of historical information current at the present day.

1. Biographical Data in Ancient Literature

As a matter of fact, very little personal history—biography or autobiography—has come down to us from the ancient world. Even letters are very scarce. The paucity of such records is one of the factors which make the writing of ancient history far more difficult than the writing of modern; it also accounts for the wide divergence in the interpretation of ancient characters, such as Alexander or Augustus, not to mention Julius Caesar. In the ancient Near and Middle East, as Hermann Bengtson has pointed out in his *Introduction to the Study of Ancient History* (3rd edition, Munich, 1959), only a few rulers, men like Hammurabi and Darius I, Cyrus and Alexander, and a few personalities from ancient Hebrew history, chiefly kings and prophets, are fairly well known. In Greek history, Hesiod—but not Homer—Archilochus, Sappho, Solon, and Pindar are among the earliest: poets, quite appropriately, not rulers, or rulers who were also poets! In Roman history, Scipio Africanus, Cato the Censor, and one or two others emerge from the mists of pre-history and legend: statesmen and soldiers, chiefly. Ample biographical material comes later, as in Cicero's letters and in Plutarch's famous *Lives*, but it is limited to a small number of subjects; the fullest are Cicero, Caesar, and the emperor Julian—still, as before, among the Romans, soldiers and statesmen.

These examples are taken chiefly from the classical world. The same conditions prevailed in the Jewish. Even the greatest saints and leaders were remembered only by a few scattered incidents and sayings—anecdotes that were told and retold in oral tradition, or favourite sayings, expositions of scripture, and especially parables or illustrative stories. The brief, pointed, proverbial sayings were often memorised by their disciples, and so were preserved to posterity. For hundreds of years this was the common method of instruction and of learning used by the Wisdom teachers and their disciples, and by the scribes and in turn the rabbis who succeeded them, during the highly literate but non-bookish era of oral tradition from Ezra to Judah the Prince. The writing down of the oral tradition was usually an afterthought, and it was not biographical: see, for example, the Wisdom of Jesus the Son of Sirach, and the traditions in the Mishnah and Talmud. Hence we must not expect too much. The gospels were written, not to provide us with biographies of Jesus, but as the church's brief records of its own beginning, at the dawn of the New Age, the era of salvation. "The beginning of the gospel" (Mark I.1) was the beginning of its *proclamation*. This was still the purpose of the latest gospel, John (see xx.31).[1]

2. The Meaning of "The Kingdom of God"

It is also true, and characteristic of ancient religious literature in general, apart from works produced in a school, that some of the greatest and most important *concepts* were not exactly defined. Hence they are not precisely definable

[1] See Ch. III of my book, *The Gospels, Their Origin and Their Growth*.

now, with the result that modern authorities (or at least modern authors!) disagree completely in their interpretation. For example, the commonest term in the gospels, "The Kingdom of God", is nowhere explained, and cannot now be exactly or exhaustively defined. The modern interpretations range all the way from a political or social Utopia to the realm of the blest in Paradise, and often they hover in the intermediate region of ecclesiastical interests: the Kingdom of God means the church, or its mission, or the slow but steady conquest of society by religious ideals, or its penetration by Christian ethics. Obviously, the term could not originally have meant all of these! And yet there was wide variety in the use of the term even in the New Testament. Different writers used it in different ways. It was of course Jesus' own term, and we wish to know where he got it, how he came to use it, what it meant before he used it, how people about him understood it, in what way he modified it, how his disciples understood it (whether correctly or not), and what special meaning—if any—he gave to it in his public or private teaching. It so happens that the term was probably more common in Galilee than elsewhere: this also interests us. Finally, its Jewish origin is evident from its non-dogmatic and popular religious significance. This is something that should warn those who use it now; it cannot be treated as if it were a modern term, into which we are at liberty to read whatever meaning we wish; or an ancient philosophical term, with mystical or metaphysical overtones. It is not Greek or Latin, Egyptian or Syrian or Babylonian, let alone ancient Indian or Chinese, but Jewish; and this severely restricts the area in which a definition is to be sought and found—if found at all. But it is not likely that any first century Jew we might have happened to meet could have told us what it meant: for Judaism was not a religion with sharply defined concepts, but of strictly defined duties, a religion of practice, without any metaphysical or theological formulations. Probably any well instructed Christian of today can tell more about the meaning of the terms commonly used in his church, such terms as Grace, Justification, Judgment, or Sacrament, than any ancient Jew could have told about the meaning of such a term as "the Kingdom of God".

It is true that the explicit term "the Kingdom of God" is not found in the Old Testament or in any other Jewish literature outside the New Testament—this will excuse the ancient Jew from the quandary in which we have just placed him. That is to say, the phrase does not occur with the precise connotations with which Christians are now familiar or with those which are found in the New Testament. Nor are the associated verbs to be found there, such as *enter, come, draw near, be instructed in, be far from* or *excluded from, be taken away, be given,* and so on. Nevertheless the idea of the Reign of God is certainly present in the Old Testament and in the old Jewish literature outside the Bible. And the precise term, *the Kingdom of God,* which in the New Testament and among the early Christians expressed this idea, was one which fitted precisely the situation in which it arose and found currency. It was in origin a quasi-political as well as a religious concept, and it entered the world of Christian literature still trailing some of the quasi-political connotations which it bore from its time and place of origin. It still bears those connotations in the teaching of Jesus, as the old evangelic tradition makes clear, though he did much to strip away the political associations and leave only the purely religious concept.

Josephus tells us repeatedly that at successive crises in the political history of the two centuries from 100 B.C. to A.D. 100, the period during which Palestine was gradually being made a part of the eastern frontier of the Roman Empire, the Jews pleaded to be set free from "the royal and other forms of [human] government, and to be allowed to serve God only" (see, for example, his *Antiquities of the Jews* XVII, 11.2=§304ff.). Neither the regal institutions of the surrounding nations, let alone the tradition of royalty from Saul to the Exile in Israel's own history, or in the history of the later Maccabees and Herod, nor the presumably representative government of republican Rome, with its dictators, triumvirates, and incessant civil strife, appealed to the Jews. Their own peculiar type of political order had already been set forth clearly in the sacred scriptures: a theocracy, with God alone as their King, his chosen priests (the family of Aaron, the tribe of Levi) the regular ministers and administrators of this order, and with occasional prophets as the extraordinary and specially chosen bearers of specific messages from God to his people. This was the heart of the conception: it was a Reign of God, rather than the reign of any earthly king—Pharaoh, or the king of Babylon, or the "Great King" of Persia, or the Roman legate or the procurator or even Caesar himself, not to mention the Roman Senate or the *Boulē* of some Greek city or the wicked rule of Herod. The term "the Kingdom of God" thus came into use (*a*) as a term for an unrealised ideal—hence its genuinely eschatological connotations. Moreover, (*b*) its underlying idea was thoroughly this-worldly: no other-worldly realm "in the skies" could have met the situation. And it was basically (*c*) a religious conception, rooted in the idea of the Covenant, and pre-supposing throughout the principle of Israel's special relation to the God of their fathers. Nevertheless, (*d*) involved in the conception were features which reflected the political experience—the long political misadventure—of Israel during the earlier centuries, especially during the period which had succeeded that of the Maccabees. "Kingdom" now meant world-empire; "of God" now meant the divine Reign in place of every earthly monarchy.

In the literature of the Old Testament, especially in that part of it which was written (or revised) after the Exile, the doctrine of the divine sovereignty is clearly set forth. God is "the king of all the earth" (Ps. XLVII.7), "of them that dwell in the ends of the earth, and in the wide sea also" (cf. Ps. CXXXIX.9). He is "loving unto every man, and his mercy is over all his works" (Ps. CXLV.9 BCP). Israel may say, "God is my king of old" (Ps. LXXIV.13), but in the time to come God will say, "Blessed be Egypt my people, and Assyria the work of my hands, and Israel my heritage" (Isa. XIX.25). This sovereignty is not the result of conquest, like that of other universal deities in the world's history, nor of election (as by choosing Israel to be his people he "made himself a name" and thus became a sovereign, their divine "lord"); instead, for the religious thinkers of Israel, God's sovereignty was the result of his work as Creator:

> The Lord sits enthroned above the water flood [the primeval chaos],
> The Lord sits enthroned as king for ever. (Ps. XXIX.10.)

It was he who "took up the isles as small dust", who "weighed the mountains in a balance" (Isa. XL.12-17). Therefore he is Lord of heaven and earth, the one and only God, and beside him there is no other (Isa. XLIII.11). It is the reign of this eternal God, whose "kingdom" or "kingship" is from everlasting, which must nevertheless "come"—be fully realised, perfectly established—here upon earth.

For as it is the paradox of all theistic religion, so it was the paradox of Israel's faith that the one and only Creator God, who is at one and the same time the Sustainer of the universe, the Judge of all mankind, the Lord of history, and the Arbiter of human destiny, is faced with a revolt within his broad empire—like the "Great King" when one or two provinces had rebelled. He will of course eventually put down this revolt; thereafter peace and security will prevail once more (cf. Zech. XIV.9). But in the meantime various forces—material, political, human, demonic—are arrayed against the King. This was the major theme, this was the central presupposition of ancient Jewish apocalyptic, which the early Christians took over. The present hour, for the early Christians, was the *Zwischenzeit* between the beginning of the revolt and its suppression—or rather, between the beginning of the reconquest and its final glorious termination, when sin shall cease, and "there shall be no more death" (Rev. XXI.4); when "the kingdoms of this world become the kingdom of our Lord [God] and of his Christ" (Rev. XI.15); when "the last enemy, Death, being destroyed, the Son shall yield up the [reconquered] kingdom to the Father, that God may be all in all" (or "everything to everyone", the centre of every real existence, 1 Cor. xv.28 RSV).

3. *A Transformed Political Concept*

The Kingdom of God, then, was basically a political idea—but political in the ancient religious sense, according to which "politics" was a part of religion and expressed practically the doctrine of theodicy, God's rule of the world. (It is of interest to note that "Kingdom of God" still means theodicy, for St. Thomas and the medieval theologians.) It was this idea which Jesus made his own, the vehicle of all his teaching; which he elaborated, deepened, and surrounded with ethical and spiritual sanctions and conditions; which he identified with the purpose of God in his own time, and adopted as the clue to his own prophetic or messianic mission: he was—or was to be—God's Agent in the final establishment (re-establishment) of the divine Reign in this world. The stages in the growth of this conviction cannot be made out; the exegesis of the gospels and the writing of the life of Jesus fifty years ago read in too much of theory and interpretation into the records. Instead, the message is trumpeted in clear tones, with no preliminary overture: "The Kingdom of God is at hand: Repent and believe!" (Mark 1.14f.). Thus the Kingdom is announced—but not explained. It was the political connotations of this un-explained term "the Kingdom of God" which made possible the perverted charge (Luke XXIII.2) upon which Jesus was put to death by the Romans.

The whole of the New Testament provides the later Christian explanation, or rather a whole series of explanations. In Mark, for example, the earliest gospel, the Kingdom of God appears to be the final "eschatological" condition of the world in which the will of God has fully prevailed and the present evil world has been transformed into a world of divine power and light. Jesus' "mighty works" are the evidence of the Kingdom's approach, and of the certainty of its ultimate arrival—not "signs and wonders" (or "miracles", as we call them) but "powers of the Age to Come" (cf. Heb. VI.5) already at work in the present age. To Mark, writing for the martyr church at Rome, this was the greatest possible assurance of victory over the dark forces arrayed against the Christians, circa A.D. 68. In "Q", the early Sayings Source used by Matthew and Luke in addition to Mark,[1] the same is true: "If it is by the Spirit of God that I cast out demons, then the Kingdom of God has come upon you" (Matt. XII.28, Luke XI.20). In Luke the same view prevails. Although Luke has his eye upon the Gentile church of his own time, late in the first century, he still thinks of the Kingdom of God as the consum-mation of history, and sees the events leading up to it in the light of the ultimate realisation of the will of God—for example,

---

[1] On the gospels and their sources see my book, *The Gospels, Their Origin and Their Growth* (London, Faber and Faber, 1959), which includes an extensive bibliography, pp. 202ff.

Jerusalem "surrounded by armies" (xxi.20). In Matthew the "eschatological" emphasis is greater than in any other gospel; and yet there are passages which seem to identify the Kingdom of God with the Jewish religious institution (xxi.43), or with the divine Covenant, as if Matthew already shared the theology of far later theologians. At the same time he has passages which seem to reflect the view that the Kingdom of God is identical with the church, the institution that exists between the present time and the Last Day, or between the Resurrection and the Last Judgment (xiii.41; cf. xvi.18, the "gates of Hades", the powers of death, "shall not prevail against it"; cf. xxviii. 20). Perhaps the best explanation is that Matthew is a "traditional" book, and contains a diversity of elements, some old, some new (cf. xiii.52), some traditional, that is, derived from the early Christian Jewish community, some freshly created to meet the needs of the Hellenistic-Roman missionary field. The Apocalypse of John (Revelation) is the most extreme, even extravagant, apocalyptic interpretation of the Christian gospel; but it can scarcely be taken as a reflection of early Christian teaching or expectation as a whole, either of the Palestinian type reflected in the sources underlying the Synoptic Gospels or of the Pauline type presupposed in the theology of the majority of the early Gentile churches. In the Gospel according to John, curiously, the term "Kingdom of God" has virtually disappeared, as it has almost disappeared in the Epistles of Paul. For both Paul and John, and for most of the later New Testament writers (that is, the authors of Hebrews, the Catholic Epistles, and the Pastoral Epistles), the Person of Christ has taken the place of centrality which had formerly been occupied by the Kingdom of God in both the teaching of Jesus and the earliest gospel tradition. Here is one of the most significant facts about the rise of the Christian religion: (a) the Hellenistic-Roman world was little interested in either a this-worldly political or in a completely cosmic renewal (the Stoic metaphysics probably received little stress in their popular teaching), but (b) the Hellenistic-Roman world was deeply and increasingly interested in personal manifestations of the divine, while (c) more and more, in ever wider circles, the religious minds of that age were interested in salvation, not within the world but out of it (contrast John

XVII.15), not in political or social idealism or welfare but in individual and personal salvation.

It is scarcely possible to make out the main stages in the development of the earliest Christianity, or its varieties of expression, apart from a thorough source-analysis of the gospels, a type of inquiry which involves textual criticism, philological analysis, the study of literary style, the exact comparison of parallel passages, historical research, and eventually form criticism, which is the attempt to recover and reconstruct the underlying oral tradition. Many books have been written, setting forth various theories of the origin of the gospels or of the rise of Christianity and the development of Christian doctrine, which have ignored this simple require-ment of careful analysis of the sources—with the result that many different interpretations of the Kingdom of God have been elaborated, few of which commend themselves to the historian as probable; fewer still are mutually compatible. The manifold variety in the New Testament interpretation of the idea of the Kingdom of God is the result of the on-going religious experience and the developing thought of the earliest generations of Christians, especially as the church spread into new areas where the religious antecedents and presuppositions were totally different from those which were traditional in Jewish Palestine. If we seek a uniform, consistent, and literal record of Jesus' teachings, we shall find the gospels a collection of puzzles. Jesus' teaching, his life, death, and resurrection were basic to them—but the gospels also give us the later interpretations; and the only possible way toward a solution of these inconsistencies is a frank recognition of the variety in interpretation reflected not only by the gospels but also by their underlying sources.[1]

It was out of the great conception of the coming Reign of God, for which ancient Judaism longed and prayed ("Be thou alone Ruler over us!"—see p. 47) and which Jesus made central in his teaching, that the whole movement of primitive Christianity took shape. It is useless to undertake, at this late date in the history of modern scholarship, to show that primitive Christianity was a purely "social" movement,

---

[1] See my *Introduction to New Testament Thought*, Ch. II, "The Meaning of Growth and Variety".

inspired by the discontent of the "submerged masses" throughout the Roman Empire; or that it arose as one more philosophy
of ethical moderation and goodwill, somewhat like Stoicism
or Aristotelianism, with the Golden Rule as its cardinal
principle; or that it was a kind of theosophical brotherhood
or "mystery" cult, with a simple meal of bread and wine as
its leading observance, where all shared and shared alike; or
that the Kingdom of God really meant Utopia and the brotherhood of man. These outmoded and now impossible interpretations have nothing to offer in lieu of the obviously sound and
correct view that Christianity arose as a purely Jewish religious
movement, and that its concepts, ideas, hopes, and aspirations
must be interpreted in the light of its basically Jewish nature,
character, antecedents, and outlook. The Kingdom of God,
in the New Testament period, was still the old prophetic
dream of the complete and perfect realisation, here upon
earth, of the sole sovereignty of the one and only God:

> Our Father, who art in heaven,
>   Hallowed be thy name;
> Thy Kingdom come,
> Thy will be done,
>   On earth as it is in heaven.

4. *The Ethics of the Kingdom of God*

But the main difficulty with Jesus' teaching, for many
persons, is not his eschatology, his belief in the immediate
coming of the Last Days, the final Judgment and the establishment of the Reign of God "on earth as in heaven"; instead,
it is his *ethics*. Some persons have a positive aversion for
"ethics", which seem to them a purely academic and theoretical
analysis of human conduct and motives, abstract and unreal,
cold and impersonal, and utterly incapable of inspiring the
love of goodness, righteousness, or obedience to the will of
God. Others detest all rules designed to regulate conduct,
and view "morals" and "moralism" as inseparable, and
designed only to win merit—as if anyone who kept the law
must be guided by his own self-interest in doing so, either to
escape prison or to win public approval, influence, or praise.
But the criticism of "moralism" is equally academic: people

K

are not controlled as mechanically and automatically as the critics suppose! Human motives are often deep and complicated, and represent a convergence of many interests, among which self-regard is only one.

Now it is clear that in Jesus' teaching, and in most of the New Testament, the "ethics" are closely related to the message of the Kingdom of God. If God's Kingdom is about to appear, or to be set up, or to be perfectly established; and if men are to be admitted to it as members, or as citizens, or as loyal subjects; then two things are necessary: repentance (Mark I.15) and the actual practice of the new righteousness (Matt. VI.33), which is superior to that taught and exemplified by the scribes (*ib*. v.20, XXIII.3). For the Reign of God is of such a nature that only those who obey and respond to the will of God can be admitted—or allowed to remain—within the blessed realm (*ib*. XIII.41, 43, 49). At this point arises the purely modern problem: was Jesus' "ethics" meant for all mankind, or only for Jews, or only for his own followers, or only for the elect—who were required to live by the standards of the coming Kingdom here and now, in advance of its arrival? In brief, was it, as Albert Schweitzer holds, an "interim ethic", a high, heroic code meant for the shock troops, the commandos, the expendables, the guerrilla fighters of the coming divine monarchy—and not at all a system of ethics for all mankind?

The situation is much like that found in the earlier stages of all ancient law, which was sacred, inspired, and based upon religious ideas: for example, the religious Law set forth in the Jewish Torah, or the Code of Hammurabi, or the "laws of the kings" surviving in republican Rome. In Jesus' teaching there was no philosophical analysis of right or duty or personal relations or the state, but simply the direct religious appeal to be good as God is good, to be like God, to be "perfect" as he is perfect (Luke VI.36, Matt. V.48). Viewed as a system of ethics, to be embraced under one universal principle—such as love, or likeness to God, or the rule of his Kingdom, or the demands of discipleship—the teaching seems heterogeneous, like almost all ancient religious and moral teaching. Even the highly developed and carefully articulated Roman Law, as historians remind us, cannot be bracketed under one major principle, but implies several.[1] And—at least at first glance—the early Christian ethics, especially as set forth in the Gospel of Matthew, appear likewise to be a more or less accidental combination of heterogeneous elements. Asceticism, self-denial, abnegation, the heroic ethics of martyrdom are found side by side with the ethics of revolt against religious reaction and tyranny—but not against political. Shrewd common sense or everyday prudence is invoked side by side with the hope of heaven and the beatific vision. Cynical worldly-wise aphorisms (e.g. Matt. vi.34b) are cited along with appeals to the utmost self-giving; utter hatred of hypocrisy alternates with ardent love of neighbour, even of enemy. Moreover, the emphasis and proportion of the ethics vary from gospel to gospel. Obviously there must be more than one source for this complex motivation and changing emphasis. The ethics of the gospels, like the rest of their teaching, is traditional: Jesus' teaching has been handed down orally, has been interpreted, explained, and applied by the teachers of the early church who were its custodians and stewards. Like the scribes who taught the Torah (Matt. xxiii.2), the church's teachers handed on a tradition, and brought out of their treasure "what is new and what is old" (*ib*. xiii.52).

Modern research has shown that the idea of the coming Reign of God, the divine King who is also his people's earthly sovereign, the dream of a true *regnum dei in terra*, is very old, and long antedates the Christian religion. It rests ultimately upon the profound conviction that God alone is the Creator and Sustainer of the universe, and that his will must eventually prevail everywhere. The term "the Kingdom of God" is rare in ancient Jewish literature, probably for the reason that it became—or implied—the slogan of the Zealots: "No king but God". Jesus rescued it from its revolutionary connotations, and made it central in his teaching. But he nowhere defined it. One must gather its meaning from the gospels as a whole, from his teaching as a whole, and from the course of his life and the later spread of the church. Its profoundest connotations are the identity of the Reign of God with the final purposes

---

[1] See W. W. Buckland, *Roman Law from Augustus to Justinian* (Cambridge, 2nd ed., 1932), p. xi.

of God the Creator and Redeemer, and with the manifestation of his real character, his wisdom, power, justice, and love, his infinite compassion, his ready forgiveness, his unwearying patience, his unfathomable longing and affection for his children, even when they wander away, his utter self-giving, self-outpouring concern for those he loves. What Jesus did was set this conception of God at the very heart of the idea of the coming Kingdom. Thus he neutralised its political and revolutionary connotations and transformed the idea into a purely religious, immeasurably dynamic conception.

The Jewish features in this conception, both of God the Father and his coming Reign, are unmistakable, undeniable. When the church took over the idea it inclined to shift it back into the framework of either political eschatology (as in the Apocalypse of John) or the general cosmological eschatology which eventually triumphed and became the traditional "doctrine of the last things". Even so, its fundamentally religious character was never lost. To the medieval Schoolmen (see p. 123), the Kingdom of God was not the church, nor the transformed world after the Day of Judgment, nor "heaven" (as opposed to "earth"), but the everlasting Reign of God over the entire universe, the divine theodicy. This was not Jesus' conception, but it was closely allied to it—a philosophical equivalent, one might say. And it certainly expressed the fundamental religious conviction which lay at the heart of the concept, for both Judaism and Christianity, as may be seen from the 145th Psalm.

CHAPTER NINE

The Jesus of History

Three important factors are involved in the historical study of any great figure in the past, including the figure of Jesus: his background, his surroundings, and his own purpose and aims. These of course do not include all of the factors, nor do they presuppose a deterministic view of history; nor, let us say at once, do they define in advance the meaning which any man (Jesus included) is to have for later history, for the religious or the intellectual, the political or the social life of later generations.

By the *background* we mean, in the case of Jesus, his ancestry, his religious heritage, the living tradition of worship, religious ideas, customary practices, and daily piety which was found in post-exilic Judaism, especially in the important period of the great Tannaim. All this was concentrated in the religion and worship of the synagogue, with its inspiring prayers, its noble ethical teaching, its sacred scriptures, its sublime hope of things to come. By the *surroundings* we mean, in this case, the political and social conditions amid which Jesus grew to manhood and fulfilled his life's mission. This included, chiefly, the steadily increasing Roman occupation of Palestine from the days of Herod onwards, and the growing opposition, not only by the Zealots but by others. The result was a religious tension which resulted in heightened apocalyptic hopes, on the one hand, and in movements of world-renunciation, on the other—like the one that produced the so-called Essene community at Qumrân near the Dead Sea. By the *purpose and aims* of Jesus we mean something more than simply his "reaction to the situation" in which he found himself. Most men, it is true, merely "react"; creative personalities do more—they change the conditions, they open new doors and vistas, they mark out new paths, they lead in new directions; and so they set men free from the *impasse* into which the course of events has driven them. This was surely true of Jesus. The alternatives which he faced are pictured symbolically in the narrative of his Temptation in the Wilderness, with which the Synoptic Gospels begin. The way which he chose led inevitably to defeat and death—as the evangelists surely realised. But his defeat and death were only preliminary to his victory—as all the gospels, especially John, and Paul, and indeed the whole New Testament, and the whole course of early Christian history, bear witness. This is the pattern or "frame" in which the life of Jesus is set by our earliest records—the only "records" we possess.

1. *Can the Life of Jesus be Written?*

One may, of course, go behind all this and say, "We cannot possibly make out a real historical person, or an authentic historical career, from such biased, theologically motivated records as these!" Indeed, many persons at the present time have drawn precisely this conclusion. And they are not all "sceptics and unbelievers"—some of the most orthodox among us hold this view. They fill the blank space in first-century history by inserting a purely theological figure, one which is divine and non-human, for all their theological insistence upon "the reality of his human nature". The church's long struggle to maintain the balance of scripture, and to assert both the deity and the humanity of Jesus Christ has never really come to an end; people still think of him as one or the other, God or man, since the combination is an inconceivable "mystery". But that is exactly what the church has called it, the "mystery" of the Incarnation.

But historians, including historical interpreters of the New Testament and other documents of the early church, exegetes, historians of doctrine, and likewise students of the history of religion as a whole, cannot fill a blank space with a non-human, purely supernatural figure, in the way the ancient Docetists and Gnostics did, or as many other persons, unconcerned with historical problems, still endeavour to do. It is the glory and the strength of the Christian religion that it takes history seriously. As Christians, therefore, not as "secular" historians (if there really are any such persons; many claim the title!), we must press on toward the goal, and try to make out the lineaments of the historical figure of Jesus. How did he appear to the men of his own time? To his disciples? To his neighbours and friends? To his enemies? To the ecclesiastical authorities and the religious leaders? To the men in the Roman army of occupation?—Answers to these questions are at least clearly hinted in the gospels.

It makes no difference that dozens of different "reconstructions" have already appeared, from solid historical investigations to the most airily fanciful of fictions. One may read about them in Albert Schweitzer's *Quest of the Historical Jesus* or in Chester McCown's *Search for the Real Jesus*. Such variety of interpretation was inevitable, in view of the scanty records, and especially in view of the equally scanty knowledge of first century Palestine, both Jewish and Roman, on the part of many modern writers. Sometimes this ignorance has been made worse by bitter—often unconscious—prejudice, not only against Judaism, or against Christianity, but against Roman civilisation, or against theology, or even against religion in general.

The way in which prejudice works can easily be illustrated from many of the so-called "Lives of Jesus" written since the eighteenth century. It may also be illustrated from the preposterous inferences and hypotheses which many persons have advocated since the Dead Sea Scrolls were discovered— inferences which sometimes openly betray their propounders' unfamiliarity with ancient Judaism as well as with New Testament history and exegesis. A thorough training in historical interpretation is not to be acquired by reading a few good books *about* the subject, but only by devoting years of patient study to the sources for the history. Always the sources, the sources—first, last, and all the time! Anyone can now read the Dead Sea Scrolls, in the original or in translation; anyone can read the Gospel of John; but one must know thoroughly many more books, both ancient and modern, before he ventures to affirm the dependence of one upon the other. The journalists of course do not realise this, nor do many of the laity, some of whom try to make John the earliest of the gospels, for obvious apologetic reasons. But the more learned scholars do not share the bizarre interpretations current in many circles—views which make John the Baptist, or even Jesus, a member of the "Essene" group or even of the Qumrân community, and the author of the Gospel of John a doctrinaire Qumrân theologian.

Yet in spite of the mutually contradictory "Lives of Jesus" that have appeared since the eighteenth century, and in spite of the strange misconceptions of early Christianity and of Judaism, or of the character and purpose of Jesus himself, or of the gospel records, we still believe it is possible to trace the general outlines of the life and the career, the teaching and the personality of Jesus of Nazareth.

2. *The Sources for the Life of Jesus*

The sources for the life of Jesus are those found in the four gospels, chiefly the Synoptics; and by sources I mean those which underlie the gospels—in the Synoptics, L, Q, Mark, and M, together with the editorial additions and alterations made by the evangelists.[1]   Underlying even our earliest gospel, that of Mark, there are older sources, "sequences" of tradition, little collections of related material (e.g. the parables in ch. IV or the apocalyptic sayings in ch. XIII), and longer narratives (e.g. the old Roman Passion Narrative underlying chapters xiv-xv).[2]   Unquestionably, historical materials also underlie John, though the tradition has sometimes been modified and revised much more thoroughly than most of the tradition in the Synoptics.   For example, the Passion Narrative of John contains features that look more "primitive" than those of the Synoptic Passion Narratives, than even Mark's; the cleansing of the Temple may have come earlier in Jesus' ministry than the Synoptists (following Mark) assume; the messianic acclamation at the Entry into Jerusalem may have been, as John describes it, a spontaneous demonstration by an enthusiastic crowd of pilgrims, and not the prearranged event which Mark describes (Matthew and Luke merely follow Mark).   These are items in the interpretation and writing of the historical life of Jesus which are of first-rate importance, and must be taken

[1] See my book, *The Gospels, Their Origin and Their Growth* (Faber and Faber, 1959).

[2] See my book, *The Earliest Gospel* (New York, Abingdon-Cokesbury, 1943), Ch. VIII.

into careful account by the present-day student. The long reign of the "Marcan hypothesis" is over—that is, the late nineteenth century preference for Mark above all other gospels, and the assumption that everything in Mark was absolutely trustworthy and beyond question.

Attempts have been made now and then to recover additional sayings of Jesus, or incidents in his life, from the Apocryphal Gospels, or from the "floating tradition" found here and there in the writings of the church fathers, in the papyri, and in the variant readings of certain New Testament manuscripts. One of the most wide-ranging is a recent Penguin book, *Beyond the Gospels*, by Roderic Dunkerley (1957). Here even the traditions of Islam are ransacked for surviving sayings of Jesus—and even the modern apocrypha, purely and self-evidently fictitious, are examined! To these I might add another title, *Il Primo Evangelo: La Vita di Gesu' Nazareno scritta da Giuseppe di Gerusalemme, suo Discepolo*, copyrighted in 1928 by Salvatore Riggi and printed at Schenectady, New York, with a preface by Luigi Moccia. It is a strange little book: Jesus is born, e.g., under "Archelaus, the ethnarch of Judea and son of Herod". It contains much of the gospel tradition—but other things as well, e.g. (ch. xvii) Jesus' rebuke of a man for beating an ass: "Do not mistreat any animal, nor burden them overmuch, seeing that they are God's creatures." If you have ever seen the poor donkeys in Sicily, over-burdened and beaten, or heard them braying in protest, you will perhaps rejoice that the good missionary included this story in the *Evangelo* which he distributes to his hearers. Dean Inge once observed that inhumanity to animals is conspicuously a Mediterranean vice. If ever a moral or religious need created a saying, this is an example.[1]

---

[1] I wish the same could be said for the newly recovered Gnostic sayings, in the so-called *Gospel of Thomas* found at Nag Hammadi in Egypt. Unfortunately, the new ones are the worst of the lot and the most improbable. See *The Secret Sayings of Jesus*, by Robert M. Grant and David Noel Freedman, a critical edition with introduction and commentary based on an accurate and readable translation by William R. Schoedel (New York, Doubleday, 1960 ; London and Glasgow, Collins, "Fontana Books", 1960) ; see also Jean Doresse, *L'Evangile selon Thomas, ou les paroles secrèts de Jésus* (Paris, Plon, 1959). The Coptic text is edited with translation in *The Gospel According to Thomas* (Leiden, Brill, 1959 ; New York, Harpers, 1959). This is a joint work of five scholars: A. Gillaumont, H.-Ch. Puech, G. Quispel, W. Till, and Yassah 'abd al Masīḥ.

But where are we to stop, in our search for material on the life of Jesus? To some readers, fiction is more impressive than history, and a novel like *The Robe* moves them far more deeply than the New Testament. Such persons prefer a lively journalistic paraphrase to a faithful translation of the Bible text. Of course there is a place for paraphrase—but let us call it that, as the Scots Psalter does. And there is also a place for religious fiction; but let us call it that and not let anyone think we are substituting fiction for fact, or a modern imaginative interpretation for the work of the evangelists. I say this realising full well that the evangelists likewise give us interpretation, and that sometimes, in fact often, we must go behind the first century interpretation (as also behind the twentieth century interpretation) to the first century tradition; and back of the first century tradition to the first century facts.[1] None of this work has been done for us, as lazy readers would like to assume; we must do it for ourselves. And we must not be deterred by those persons, earnest, devout, and sincere as they are, who have simply no interest in historical questions, or for whom the past does not really exist, and who bid us "take the Bible as it is" and stop trying to get behind its plain statements and meaning. Alas, we cannot! For the scripture itself bids us "search and see", and invites the historian's attention by its very claim to contain historical material. If our religion were purely metaphysical and non-historical, like Hinduism, we might pick its doctrines out of thin air, and put them together into a rational system, with little or no reference to history. But Christianity is a historical religion, and demands historical recognition and accounting. It is no system of metaphysical categories cruising aloft in search of some clear and level place for a safe three-point landing in history, say in the life of Jesus of Nazareth. Instead, to change the figure, it is ploughed deep into the soil of human life, and comes to us redolent of the freshly upturned earth in ancient Galilee. An unhistorical Christianity, say one of the old Gnostic systems or some modern Manichean or Gnostic revival, is no longer Christianity, or even religion at all, but speculation—as we view it. One may at the same time go

---

[1] See my paper, "The Authenticity of Jesus' Sayings" in *Neutestamentliche Studien für Rudolf Bultmann* (Berlin, Töpelmann, 1954; 2nd ed., 1957), pp. 137-143.

farther back, and raise the prior question—with the old Attic orator Andocides: "Is it really necessary to speculate about matters relating to the gods?" (*On the Mysteries*, §139).[1] We would not forbid theological speculation; but it is no substitute for historical research, exegesis, or literary analysis. It seems to me that during the past forty years, or since the end of World War I, a black cloud of anti-historical dogmatism has drifted across the sky, blotting out the stars. But if Christianity ever gives up history, its own history, or ceases to take history seriously and comes to view it as mere legend or even myth, it will simply cease to be Christianity. For it will have renounced its most distinctive characteristic, by which it has been known for almost twenty centuries.

3. *Jesus' Background*

The life of Jesus was lived within narrow boundaries of space and time. Palestine was a small country. The distance from Nazareth in Galilee to Jerusalem in Judea was scarcely seventy-five miles. From Capernaum to Tyre was forty; to Caesarea Philippi twenty-five. Jesus never saw Rome or Alexandria or Antioch or Ephesus, the great cosmopolitan "centres of civilisation" in his day. And the brief span of his life extended only from the latter days of Herod (who died in 4 B.C.) to the procuratorship of Pontius Pilate (who governed Judea and Samaria from A.D. 26 to 36). The traditional dates, 4 B.C. for his birth, A.D. 29 or 30 for his death, make his lifetime one of the briefest in all the great biographies of the past. Other men take far longer, as a rule, to accomplish their ends, or to make their impact on the world. Only a few, the poet John Keats, the composer Franz Schubert, one or two others, come to mind as comparable.

The story of his birth, as we have seen, is enshrined in two groups of beautiful legends, and it is told from the messianic viewpoint by both Luke and Matthew, the only evangelists who tell it. Behind these legends are the earnest hopes and expectations of those among whom Jesus grew up. The story of his journey to Jerusalem at the age of twelve (Luke II.41-52) is like the "pronouncement stories" found later on in the

---

[1] Compare the Christian apologist, Minucius Felix, *Octavius*, VI.I.

narratives of his ministry, or like the "apothegms" of the
fathers, the saints and teachers of religion: its whole point is
the saying, "How is it that you sought me? Did you not know
that I must be in my Father's house?"—a beautiful expression
of pure childlike faith. We should only spoil the story if we
began raising questions about its authenticity, its probable
sources, its theological implications, and so on.

At this point something must be said about the poetic
element in the gospel tradition as a whole. We do not need
to "demythologise" it—but only to "deliteralise" our interpretation of it and recognise its poetic, symbolic, non-literal
character and its permanent spiritual meaning. Much of
Jesus' teaching was set forth in parables that conveyed his
message in words men could not help but remember. He did
not only say, "You must seek first God's kingdom, before
everything else" (cf. Matt. vi.33); he told a story about a
pearl-buyer who found somewhere "the pearl of great price"
and invested everything he possessed in its purchase, and
another about a man who came upon a treasure—perhaps a
coin hoard—hidden in a field, and promptly bought the piece
of land in order to claim its jar of gold (cf. Matt. xiii.44-46).
He not only, like the apostle, enjoined men to "pray constantly"
(cf. 1 Thess. v.17); he also told stories of incessant prayer—the
woman crying out for justice to a busy or indifferent judge
(Luke xviii.2ff.), the late-arriving guest whose host found
himself short of bread (Luke xi.5-8)—stories that are sometimes
tragic, sometimes humorous, but always homely in their
settings and motivation. He used hyperboles: a man with
a timber in his eye who could scarcely see well enough to remove the fleck of sawdust in his brother's eye (Luke vi.41f.);
wolves prowling in sheepskins—a rather poor disguise (Matt.
vii.15); a woman sweeping her whole house to find one lost
coin (Luke xv.8); a camel (or even a "cable", in the Armenian
version) squeezed through a needle's eye (Matt. xix.24)—
these are gigantic comedy-figures, they are *meant* to be monstrous
and grotesque. The humour is like Lincoln's, or Swift's, or the
satire of Rabelais—peasant humour, the kind that created
Paul Bunyan and his great Blue Ox; but with a difference,
for Jesus' humour is made to serve an intensely serious religious
message, the repentance men must manifest before they can

think of entering the coming Reign of God. The figures are mostly from village life, or rural; they are taken from the familiar scenes about him, from the people he knew, the people his hearers knew. And so are the reflections of nature. The lilies of the field (Matt. vi.28) still bloom in all their gorgeous colour on the hillsides of Galilee; they "neither spin nor weave", and yet Solomon in all his glory was "not arrayed like one of these". Jesus had an eye for the beauties of nature; but he was no nature-poet, revelling in sunsets, for he had the peasant's concern for rain and fair weather (Matt. xvi.2f.; Luke xii.54f.), and his chief interest, in looking at the wild lilies, was the divine providence: "If God so clothes the grass . . ., how much more will he clothe you, O men of little faith!" (Luke xii.28). The poetry of the gospels, their use of imagery, their appeal to men's imagination, is religious, from beginning to end. It would ruin this poetry to ask pedestrian "scientific" or theological questions, or try to force a dogmatic or even a psychological interpretation upon it. "The Kingdom of God comes not with observation" (Luke xvii.20: i.e. "with signs to be observed", RSV): its signs can be understood only by those who are waiting for it in faith and hope—not by astrologers, numerologists, or apocalyptic schemers with their "days of years" and their "times" and "half-times".

4. Jesus the Teacher and Healer

The Jesus of history was a new and different kind of teacher than men in first-century Palestine were accustomed to—or men anywhere, at any time. He was not a rabbi: there were no "rabbis" in his time, but only scribes and priests. He certainly was no philosopher, as writers in the *Aufklärung* loved to think, or a "founder" of a new religion, as the nineteenth century "comparative religionists" tried to make out. He was a Galilean Jew from a small town named Nazareth. Like many Jews, ancient and modern, he was a deep student of the sacred scriptures—he knew them from beginning to end. When he criticised them (as no other Jew in his circle ventured to do) he appealed from one passage to another, from Deuteronomy to Genesis, from Moses' concession of divorce to God's intention of monogamy (Mark x.2-9). When he criticised the traditional ethic and its interpretation, he appealed to the fundamental principle or real purpose in the ancient legislation (for example the laws concerning murder, oaths, adultery, retaliation, in Matt. v.17-48). The modern dogmatic theological exegesis which reads these passages as his own authoritative pronouncement, "You have heard that it was said, so-and-so, but *I* say to you", as if he were thus emphasising his right to reformulate the Law, is quite mistaken. The wrong word is emphasised; it is not "*I* tell you", but "I *tell* you". See, for example, Matt. vi.29, Luke xii.27, just quoted, where Jesus says, "I *tell* you, even Solomon in all his glory was not arrayed like one of these". Here an emphasis on the personal pronoun would make the sentence ridiculous— the whole point is that, as everyone realises, the lilies are gorgeously beautiful—but not everyone thinks of the divine care that created them, and also us.[1]

This wholly religious orientation, this total devotion and consecration of Jesus' mind and will to the purposes of God, can nowhere better be seen than in his own view of his miracles. We must realise that "miracle" is only *our* word for it, and emphasises the wonder, the unnaturalness, even the improbability of the occurrence. But in the Bible, both in the Hebrew Old Testament and the Greek New Testament, and certainly for Jesus himself, this was not the emphatic or even the important thing—he was no thaumaturge, making a living by the trade, as adverse critics ever since Celsus have affirmed. For Jesus, these were *dunameis*, "mighty works", that is, mighty works of *God*, demonstrations of divine power, the proof of the approach of God's Reign, "the powers of the Age to Come" (Heb. vi.5) already manifest in this present age. His views were stated in the controversy with the Jerusalem scribes who "came down", perhaps to investigate his movement (Mark iii.22-27; cf. Luke xi.15-22; Matt. xii.24-29). They said, "He casts out demons by Beelzebul, the prince of demons"— an ancient pagan deity, now a "faded god" who survived as a powerful local demon, a chief of demons with an army at

---

[1] We cannot accept the explanation that "I say to you" is only the language of M, the source Matthew is using from v.8 onwards. The words are in both Luke and Matthew, as here, and represent not a stylism of M or Q, but of both: it goes back to Jesus—that is the way he talked.

his command. To the scribes, Jesus was a magician with unusual supernatural powers due to his collusion with this powerful "control" in the invisible world. Or possibly he was a Faustian figure, one who had sold his soul to Satan for ultimate delivery at death, and in return enjoyed temporary success as an exorcist in Galilee. But Jesus refuted the charge with masterly logic.

(1) If Satan thus casts out Satan, his kingdom is obviously divided in civil war, and is about to fall.

(2) If I cast out demons by Beelzebul, by whom do your sons—your disciples—cast them out? Let them judge, for the implication of your charge includes them as well!

(3) If a robber baron's castle is being ravaged and his prisoners released, obviously the robber has been disarmed and bound. Satan's power is on the wane, the "strong man" has been overcome, the day of liberation has arrived!

(4) And if it is by the finger of God—or by God's Spirit—that I cast out demons, then it is clear that the kingdom of God has come upon you, the Reign of God has arrived, it is about to begin, it is already beginning!

In a word, Jesus' whole view of the "miracles" is that they are signs of the on-coming power of God and of the establishment of his Reign, proofs of the end of the old era of sin, Satan, and death, and evidence of the inauguration of the glorious New Age. His view was what we call "eschatological", and it was purely religious. No such questions were asked, or could be asked, as the following: "Does he not possess a powerful personality, magnetic and dominant, and hence is able to suggest exorcism and liberation from demons to his hearers—who of course only think themselves possessed by them, anyway?" Or, "Do you believe there are such creatures as demons?" Or, "Is there really a devil?" Or, "How can miracles happen in a universe of law and order?" Or, "Are these not mere legends that have grown up around the life of a popular religious leader?"—the sort of thing that often happened in the ancient world, especially in the East. Such questions are remote from the scene, and would have been scouted by Jesus' immediate hearers and followers. It was not unusual for religious teachers to "do signs", such as heal the sick, exorcise demons, and do other wonderful things. It was so

unusual for John the Baptist not to do signs that people com-
mented upon it (John x.41). The idea that the ancient rabbis
did no miracles, but were simple legalists and naturalists, like
the seventeenth and eighteenth century "philosophers", is un-
founded. Paul Fiebig collected a whole volume of *Jüdische
Wundergeschichten* (1911), and as late as the Polish Chassidim
of a century and a half ago, those spiritual leaders were also
healing the sick, exorcising demons, and working wonders.
The cold "scientific" rationalist will never understand what
Jesus' ministry was like, for he—like the dogmatic theologian
—wants it to be different than it was. So too with the interpretation of Jesus' "claims"—to deity, to divinity, to Messiahship
either present or future. These "claims" have been made in
his name by his later followers, and the later the more grandiose
and unhesitating. But he himself did not make them. And the
popular dilemma of the apologists, three generations ago,
Aut deus aut homo non bonus: Either he was God, or he was not
a good man (because he made false claims), has no warrant in
the oldest tradition underlying the gospels.

Nor was he a "social radical", perhaps a Zealot, or a secret
sympathiser if not a volunteer in the "War of the Sons of Light
against the Sons of Darkness" described in one of the Qumrân
documents. If anything is certain from all the gospels, it is
that Jesus was not a revolutionist. "Render to Caesar what
is his"—it is not much, a few denarii; "Render to God what
is his"—the whole of life, the total devotion of your hearts, all
that you have and are and aspire to be! (Mark xii.17; see
p. 177). The saying in Matthew (xxvi.52), "All who take the
sword will perish by the sword", may be apocryphal, or a
current proverb, or—quite possibly—a saying of Jesus. It
fits the tenor of his other sayings. The story of the Workers in
the Vineyard (Matt. xx.1-16) is no programme for equalising
wages; it is a story to illustrate the goodness of God, who
generously gives "to this last" whether he deserves it or not.
The saying in Mark (iv.25), "To him who has will more be
given", is often viewed as a cynical comment on capitalism.
But it was only an assurance that the careful student, who
remembers and practises what he has been taught, will learn
more—a wonderful motto for a student, and profoundly
true.

5. Why did Jesus die?

Why then did Jesus die on a cross, if he was only a mild Jewish lay teacher and prophet, a healer and exorcist, who "went about doing good", and, like his earliest followers, lived "in favour with God and all the people" (Acts x.39; ii.22, 47; cf. Luke ii.52)—one who never roused any public opposition beyond the quite understandable jealousy of the scribes, those professional leaders who looked upon themselves as the authorised and official teachers of Israel? In order to answer this question we must take into account several factors which are supplied by the history and circumstances of Jesus' time. In the first place, it must be recognised that he was put to death by the Romans. Crucifixion was a Roman penalty, not a Jewish. In a period of turbulent political and social unrest; among a people who refused to acknowledge the lawfulness of Roman occupation and rejected alien sovereignty on many grounds, but chiefly religious; under a corrupt and vacillating foreign military administration, which steadily became ever more corrupt and barbarous until the oppressed nation broke out in total revolt in the year 66; in an era when "quisling" leaders—chiefly among the Sadducean hierarchy—were doing their best to maintain liaison with the Romans, and unhesitatingly handed over those who criticised or opposed them to be executed on whatever charges promised to be most effective; in a situation in which an independent religious leader, John the Baptist, had already been executed on suspicion of planning a revolt, by an arbitrary pro-Roman tetrarch, Herod Antipas; at a time when the popular mind was disturbed and "ready for any innovation", as Josephus says, prepared to accept any proposal that promised freedom or a return to the "good old days" of simple faith and piety and of consequent divine protection; among a people whose religious leaders tended more and more toward a merely casuistic, legalistic interpretation of Judaism—in a situation like this, such a person as Jesus was foredoomed to rejection and death; these are the factors that led inevitably to his execution on a trumped-up charge of fomenting revolution.

We have three separate accounts of his trial (in Mark xv.1-20, Luke xxiii.1-5 [6-12] 13-25, John xviii.19-24, 28-40,

L

xix.1-16; Matthew merely reproduces Mark). From these three accounts it is obvious that Jesus was put to death as a claimant to the vacant throne of David, as "King of the Jews", that is as the "Anointed" or "Messiah" who was to come in the great age of Israel's political restoration "in the latter days". By the Romans, this supposed claim was quite naturally interpreted as a tocsin of revolt. Many another leader in those dark days had claimed to be "King" or "Prophet" or "Messiah" (the terms overlapped), and had paid for his temerity with his own blood and that of his followers. John the Baptist had been accused of fomenting—at least of threatening, or of planning—a revolution (cf. Josephus, *Antiquities*, xviii.5.2= §§116-119), and he had been beheaded. Could a prophet perish "away from Jerusalem"? (Luke xiii.33). Obviously, the answer was *yes*; for John had been executed at Machaerus, the Perean fortress east of the Dead Sea. But the threat of disaster now hung all the more ominously over anyone who earned either the disapproval and antagonism of the Jewish hierarchy or the suspicion and surveillance of the Roman military power. Jesus apparently was fully aware of the dangers confronting him on his "march to Jerusalem", when he set his face sternly to meet his destiny (Mark x.32). All four gospels insist that he knew he was facing death—as a real prospect, something more than a mere possibility. And yet he went forward, unhesitatingly. *Why?* we ask. For the same reason that a bomber crew or a commando squad sets out, perfectly aware that they may not return; after two missions, or ten, or twenty, their prospects of survival grow less each time. But they do not think of this—only of their duty and the task in hand. I believe we can understand Jesus better by contemplating the fearless, unhesitating courage of those young men who gave their lives in battle, not long ago, to save our world from tyranny and servitude.

On the other hand, the idea that Jesus went to Jerusalem in order to die, as the final act in his fore-ordained role, seems to make him a suicide—which is something quite contrary to his whole mental and spiritual outlook. From the incident of the Temptation onward, if that symbolic story means anything at all, he had flatly refused to force the hand of God (*pace* Albert Schweitzer). The idea that he went to Jerusalem "to

fling down a challenge to the nation, assembled for the annual
Passover festival", and thus demand acceptance of himself as
its leader, is equally out of harmony with his whole ethos and
outlook on life. Self-assertion, self-aggrandisement, self-
proclamation were totally opposed to his aim, his method, his
faith in God. (See Matt. xii.18-21, quoted from Isa. xlii.1-4.)
The idea that the central concept in his message was his own
messiahship does not tally with the earliest historical sources
for his life and thought. He was a prophet and teacher; and
if, in the final denouement he was to be God's Agent in the
character of Messiah, that was entirely in God's hands, and
he would not claim the office or its responsibilities. The picture
Paul draws in Phil. ii.5-11 is as true of the historical Jesus as
it was of the cosmic, pre-existent Christ, who "did not count
equality with God a thing to be grasped"—that is, something
to be snatched or seized, a *harpagmos*, as Satan or the Titans
had attempted to dethrone God and seize the throne of the
universe; instead, he "emptied himself", stripped himself bare
of all divine privileges and prerogatives, "taking the form of
a slave", and dying "on a cross". If he refused to claim deity,
he certainly would have refused to claim messiahship—which
after all was only a quasi-political office in the historical order,
reflecting Israel's dreams of world-dominion in a coming era
of idyllic bliss.

The fact that he died unjustly, at the hands of an alarmed
and suspicious military tyrant, by no means prevented the
further spread of his teachings—the thing has happened again
and again in the East, and elsewhere. The fate of Mani, the
founder of Manicheism; the fate of the Reformation martyrs,
or of William Tyndale, the sixteenth century translator of the
New Testament; the fate of the early Christians, beginning
with the saints and apostles, Stephen, James, Peter, Paul—and
including countless victims of mob madness, imperial despotism,
or pagan fanaticism—all these illustrate the principle still
further. As the Gospel of John sublimely states it, in words
which are placed on Jesus' own lips, "And I, when I am lifted
up from the earth"—first on the cross, and then by divine
exaltation to heaven—"will draw all men to myself" (John
xii.32). In the divine dispensation, Christ's death was not
loss, but gain. Mystics, saints, theologians have found their

own religious life to be rooted in that fact of his death, and of his victory over death; not in the cross only, but in the new life which has flowed from the exalted Lord. This is a purely transcendental experience, with a resulting concept which cannot possibly be understood or explained logically but nevertheless carries with it a profound meaning for those who can and do accept it. Theologians and psychologists have tried to rationalise it, but without success. As the old *Theologia Germanica* insists, the atonement must first be a personal experience of reconciliation with God before it can be understood as a doctrine; and however true in fact, it cannot be true "for me" until I have lived it.

6. *The Gospel Today*

Similarly the gospel of Jesus: we have tried to categorise it, analyse it, fit it into other systems—but it will not fit. We cannot shift the ethics of Jesus on to some other basis than its own foundation of Jewish confidence in God and his purposes, chiefly in his eschatological purpose of justice, righteousness, mercy and peace. Not Marxism, surely: the gospel will not rest on that base; or the theory of "the greatest good for the greatest number"; or hedonism; or naturalism; or the "success" pattern of modern capitalist propaganda; or militarism; or the "master race" theory of the "German Christians"; or Tolstoian nihilism and renunciation—the gospel will not rest secure on any of these foundations. Its only sound basis is the purely religious one, found in the Law and the Prophets of the Old Testament, and still proclaimed wherever the holy scriptures are read. It is the church's solemn duty, and it is also the church's inspiring opportunity, to return once more—and repeatedly—to the teaching and example of our Lord, and to work out once more, and now more thoroughly than ever hitherto, the application of Jesus' principles to the way of life men must live—if they are to live. In this adventurous, dangerous, threatening and destructive modern world, with all its promise, with all its inertia—social, educational, political, commercial, industrial, yes, and religious— the gospel must be applied in every area of man's activity and concern. Formulas will not do it; slogans will not help much; only the patient working out of concrete, specific plans, new laws, new methods, new patterns of life at every level—this is how the gospel must save our generation and those yet to come.

We now know much more about human nature than was known hitherto—thanks to modern studies, especially of psychoanalysis, to an improved and widespread dissemination of knowledge, and—to bitter experience. We now recognise that what is wrong in many areas of social maladjustment is not merely low wages or bad housing, but greed, improvidence, physical and mental unfitness, incompetence, racial prejudice, the inability to "live and let live". These factors—and others like them—are not subject to rational modification, but spring from far deeper levels. What is required is nothing less than a total reorientation of the individual and of the society in which he drags out his unhappy existence. But what can be done about this? Can anything be done?—or must the world still go on in its present state? For all our modern attainments in some areas, the world was probably never in a more dangerous condition than now. Alas, that religion contributes so little to change things, or rather to change men! Take racial antagonism; or over-population; or under-production; or restricted production geared to the profits of one social group; or the threat of war; or marital misery; or public miseducation and widespread ignorance; or the manipulation of prices, or of taxes, to favour the privileged—things we deny, but know to exist in every nation. Does religion really accomplish much more than alleviate the unhappiness of a few individuals? The churches, alas, cannot even agree upon programmes for social betterment, let alone co-operate in carrying them into effect. The vast potential resources of religious faith are simply not tapped, and humanity is left as it is, the wounded traveller by the roadside. But, as many of us still believe, the hope of the world is centred in the gospel of Jesus. If it could only be applied to men's need, the world might be a far fairer place for God's children to live in and grow up in. It is not by systematising some scheme of theoretical concepts, derived only in part from the teaching of Jesus, but by taking in simple earnest his own basic principles and applying them here and now, in our world, that there is hope for the future. For the gospel means the redemption of the world, not its condemnation, and the salvation of all mankind, not merely of a few chosen individuals.

Modern research has shown that the career of Jesus belongs in the milieu in which the gospels place him. It is no fairy-tale reported from some never-never land, a romantic and beautiful "isle of somewhere", and from long, long ago. The story is idealised, but only because there were ideal elements in it from the beginning, in the character of Jesus himself. He fitted his own times, he met their need, he rose above them and belongs to all times, and to all men everywhere. But he was not produced by his times, his background, or his environment. The purpose and aim of his life was creative, fresh from the mind of God. He was the one person in all human history who stood closest to God, at the very centre of our life, and who explained its meaning in language that all men everywhere can understand. We believe that his life can be written, not in complete detail but as fully as the lives of most great figures in the ancient world. And we believe that his real human character, as "the man Christ Jesus", stands out distinctly in the early sources which underlie the gospels. His authentic teaching, and authentic incidents from his life, his deepest motivations and aspirations, hopes and expectations, are reflected in these sources—though dimly, we must admit, for there is no *Journal intime de Jésus* in the gospels. The character of his teaching, his central convictions—centred in the coming Reign of God—his major ideas, his type of thought and teaching, his favourite figures of speech, symbols, and stories (for example his preference for rustic imagery and his gargantuan humour)—all this stands out unmistakably in the gospels. He was a lay teacher and *chasid*, as Rudolf Otto correctly insisted (in his book, *The Kingdom of God and the Son of Man*), a saint or holy man who healed the sick, cast out demons, and proclaimed the approaching dawn of the New Age, the Kingdom of God. But he was no apocalyptist; his real concern was men's preparation for facing the divine judgment, for entering the New Age, the Reign of God, and the standards he set were God's own demands, the everlasting requirements which confront those who would "enter into life". This is something permanent, unconditional, and entirely separable from any scheme of the "last days" or the impending final judgment. As the gospels put it, he was "a teacher come from God" who "taught the way of God in truth" (John III.2, Mark XII.14), and his "mighty works"—which were God's mighty works done through him—were evidence of the on-coming surge of divine, transforming power which would accompany God's Reign.

His death, which has been a problem from the very beginning of Christian history, is no inexplicable mystery: he was put to death by the Roman procurator of Judea for fear that he might start a revolution, and the flimsy charge against him was one which the "quisling" leaders of his own people had fabricated and reported to the Romans. And yet for us, as for the writers of the New Testament—that is to say, for all Christians—his death is nevertheless a mystery. How, in God's eternal purposes, did it ever come to pass that such a person as Jesus could be handed over to death, to the igno-minious, barbaric, agonising death of a captured bandit nailed to a cross?—like a hawk nailed to a barn, to warn away other hawks. Outside the gospels, and even to some extent within them, the question is raised and answered—in part. The answers, at first tentative, and never really final, range all the way from those in the early chapters of the Book of Acts (it was a deed of blind and stupid malice) to the profounder theology of Paul and John (God himself set him forth to die), and then on to the later classical theologies of the Atonement—though to this day no complete and final answer has ever been found. For Jesus' death is one with the whole problem of evil in human life, the problem of innocent suffering, of suffering on account of others, and for others, on their behalf and in their stead and for their sake. It is the problem of all unnecessary suffering and death, as in the wars men wage upon one another, but also in the tragic annals of peace. The cross of Christ is one with the central problem of all human life, from the Book of Job to Archibald Macleish's *J.B.*, from the murder of innocent Abel to the latest fire in the slums, which the morning paper reports in a line or two: "Three children burned to death". Yet the gospel, the life of Jesus, his death, is something more than just another illustration of the ancient problem. It throws some light upon it, but more than all, it supplies a motive and a way to eliminate much of the meaningless tragedy. For the gospel is still meant to be put in practice. What John Hutton, in memorable words, once called "the proposal of Jesus" was addressed, not to Jews only, but to all mankind.

It is when the natural setting or milieu of the story of Jesus is ignored, and his life is interpreted from a wholly Gentile point of view, that insuperable difficulties begin to arise: the Virgin Birth is treated as a literal fact (as in pagan myths and legends), the "ethics" of the gospel as a "system" and not as the corollaries of a religious proclamation of the coming Reign of God, the death of Christ as a predestined crime by his own people which was nevertheless the divinely intended saving act of God, the Resurrection as a corporeal event within the causal series of natural law (contrary to Rom. vi.9 and other passages), and so on. Perhaps we might do better to read the gospels in Hebrew, say in Franz Delitzsch's translation (in classical Hebrew), or in early Palestinian Aramaic (if such a version can be found). Then we might begin to view their contents as we do those of the Old Testament, with less literalism and with more poetic understanding and spiritual insight—and without trying to force them into the frame or pattern of some modern theological system.

Part Four

THE PRESENT OUTLOOK

CHAPTER TEN

The Church's Heritage
from Judaism

The chief outward and visible inheritance of the Christian church from ancient Judaism, next to the derivation of its existence, is of course the Bible, to which the New Testament is the Christian supplement and climax. But how did the church come into possession of its heritage? And further, what were the consequences of its acceptance of this inheritance? These are questions we must now consider.

1. *The Church Took Over the Jewish Bible*

It is a paradox to speak of a "doctrine" of scripture, as if there were one dogmatically defined or at least commonly agreed doctrine held by all Christians. This is, of course, not the case. Nor has it ever been the case. There are different degrees of canonicity—the Bible itself bears witness to this variety in evaluation. At the same time, it is true that Christians have always looked upon the Bible as a sacred book, "inspired" by God, and containing both the record of divine revelation in the past and the permanent, unchanging "word" of God to all later generations of mankind. The early Christians took over this view of the Bible from the Jews. For the church's earliest scriptures were the books of the Old Testament—chiefly in the Greek translation, since the Greek-speaking Gentile churches were soon predominant—whether with or without the various secondary writings later to be known as the Old Testament "apocrypha". To this collection of sacred books, translated into Greek, the church gradually added the Christian collection, including at first some books which were later dropped from the canon and a few which eventually disappeared and now survive only in a few fragments or as mere names.

The principle upon which books were included in the canon has sometimes been described in very theological terms. Marcion's example, we are told, was decisive, since his small and truncated collection challenged the church to draw up a more inclusive "Catholic Apostolic" list. But there were other factors of great importance in the growth of the canon, chiefly the constant and regular use of the New Testament books in public worship and instruction and in private study. The Old Testament was in use by the church from the start, and it was only natural that the Christian writings should be added to the Greek Old Testament as the Christian supplement and completion of the sacred scriptures. In fact, we find specific references in the New Testament to such early use of Christian writings, for example, Paul's epistles, and also the gospels, beginning with the earliest of them, St. Mark. Both of these contain directions for public reading (Mark xiii.14, Col. iv.16).

The principle of selection seems at first to have been simply that of widespread use and proven value in worship, instruction, and debate. But when the great Gnostic crisis arose in the second century, the church's leaders found it necessary to combat strange esoteric doctrines with the weapons of their protagonists, that is, books claiming to set forth apostolic doctrine.[1] The result was a canon or collection of gospels and epistles ("the" gospel and "the" apostle) which was non-esoteric, non-speculative, non-Gnostic, yet in which every book was ascribed to an apostolic author—or at least to a companion of the apostles, an "apostolic man".[2] Thus the inspiration of these books was readily assumed—or perhaps we should say more readily recognised—as a result of (a) their inclusion in the sacred book, already recognised as inspired, namely, the Jewish Bible which in time became, for Christians, the Old Testament, and of (b) the demand for authoritative apostolic writings with which to counteract the pseudonymous Gnostic scriptures. Without defining strictly what was meant by

[1] See my book, The Gospels, Their Origin and Their Growth, pp. 22ff., 159ff.
[2] The term was used by Eusebius in his Church History, ii, 17. 2.

inspiration, the church proceeded to use these books of the Old Testament, supplemented now by the early Christian epistles, homilies, gospels, and apocalypses, in the same way the Jews used the Hebrew scriptures and the Septuagint. Some doctrine of inspiration, of one kind or another, may have been implied by this procedure; more probably, it was simply the undefined common belief and attitude which prevailed throughout the ancient world, wherever sacred books were in use. Their literal meaning was the one preferred; if this was found to be either impossible or unedifying, an allegorical meaning was invented.

It is a mistake to assume that the church—or the synagogue, or any ancient religious group—proceeded formally with the development of its organisation, like modern political bodies which begin by calling together a "constitutional assembly" to draft a declaration of principles, a set of definitions, a series of by-laws, and a governing code. The most ancient church had no idea of legislating for posterity or of thinking out the presuppositions of its practice. It emerged upon the broad stage of Graeco-Roman history as one more religion of a book, indeed as an offshoot or sect of "*the* religion of the book", Judaism. This was at the time something rather new in the history of religion. The old Greek and Roman cult-religions, even the refurbished and smartly reinterpreted primitive Eastern agricultural rites which spread westward as the "mystery" religions[1]—these had no book. Only among the philosophers were sacred books in use: Epicurus's followers referred reverently to his writings, and so did the followers of Pythagoras. Students of Plato quoted his writings with devotion, and the Stoics were deeply read in Zeno, Cleanthes, and Chrysippus. There were some who quoted Homer and Hesiod almost as sacred scriptures: Maximus of Tyre, in the late second century after Christ, often quotes Homer to clinch a point, just as Paul had quoted the Septuagint, or as a Christian preacher of today quotes a verse from the Bible. And Homer's readers likewise were allegorists, for allegorism was the only method of interpretation by which the ancient reader, lacking the modern historical view of religion, or the modern historical method of criticism of religion and its traditions or of literature

[1] See my *Ancient Roman Religion*, p. xxiv.

in general, could find any spiritual or moral teaching in many of the episodes related by the poet.

2. *The Bible was Accepted as Divinely Inspired*

The early church learned allegorism, no doubt, from the Greeks, as Philo had learned it, especially from the Stoics. But the central *presupposition* of allegorism, namely, the belief in the inspiration of scripture, was not a Greek inheritance but Oriental, especially Semitic. The inspiration of the prophets was obvious; they claimed it in so many words, "Thus saith the Lord". The inspiration of the Law was equally obvious. Its whole setting was the flaming Mount and the word of the Lord to his servant Moses on Sinai. Granted that this was a later theory, or only a dramatic setting, the priestly-prophetic origin of Deuteronomy, at least, surely points toward a divine "discourse" and a code of law; and so too, far earlier, were the oracular decisions or "judgments" which had been delivered at local shrines from the time of the Hebrew invasion of Palestine, if not from a period earlier still. In fact the whole Semitic theory of law assumed a divine revelation as its source and origin. The Greeks usually named their human lawgivers, Lycurgus, Draco, Solon, Cleisthenes; but the Semites maintained that their laws had been dictated by Marduk or Yahweh. For the Jews, Moses was only "the prophet" who spoke or wrote for God. It matters little how early we date the Priestly Code (P), even making it (if we must) a survival of pre-exilic priestly rules for everyday practice; the fact remains that with Ezra and the establishment of the Second Commonwealth the Hebrew religion became a religion of a book, that is, of *the* "book of the Law" to which later were added the collected writings about or by the prophets, and finally the book of Psalms, the five Megilloth,[1] and the other writings. The purpose of this change was clear: the nation which had been destroyed, piecemeal, in 722 B.C., in 597, and in 586 had been punished for its sins. Now, under the new plan, the people were to be thoroughly instructed in the divine Law, and strictly governed by its provisions. The great characteristic principles of Judaism were to be enforced throughout the new

[1] The Song of Songs, Ruth, Lamentations, Ecclesiastes, Esther.

Commonwealth: careful observance of the Sabbath, tithes, circumcision, the ordered round of sacrifice and song in the temple, abstention from unclean food, and rigid separation from all defiling contact with idolatry—or with idolaters, including Samaritans and pagans living in Palestine. The ruthless reform of Ezra included even the divorce of Samaritan wives and their banishment from the sacred congregation of Israel. The most intransigent requirements were laid down: the man gathering sticks for fuel on the Sabbath (which was forbidden "work") was described as a horrible example of its desecration, and his judicial murder was piously approved (Num. xv.32-36).

It was one of the most dramatic moments in the history of ancient religion when, probably in the year 397 B.C., Ezra the scribe compelled the men of Judah and Benjamin, the miserable band of hardy but discouraged pioneers, to assemble at Jerusalem and stand attentively all morning in the square facing the Water Gate while he read to them "the book of the Law", presumably the whole P-Code, or perhaps most of the Pentateuch (see Neh. viii). Even more dramatic was the scene (described in Ezra x) where the men sat in the open square before the temple, trembling in the cold rain, while the reformer castigated them for their marriage with foreign women and compelled them to put away their wives. How symbolic are these scenes! The intentions of the reformer were obviously good, but the means chosen to achieve them were certainly questionable, at least from a Christian or a modern sociological point of view. The consequences were far-reaching. Judaism became a religion of prescribed ordinances, rites, ceremonies, and meticulous observance of the details of conduct as these were either laid down by or inferred from a theoretical priestly code, whose earliest elements went back to pre-history, and whose latest reflected the ingenuity of devoted priests and teachers determined to see that the whole Law should be observed by every Israelite: "Ye shall be holy as I am holy, saith the Lord" (Lev. xi.44). Israel was no longer to be a nation like the other nations of mankind, but a chosen people, called by God to inherit high and special privileges and also to carry out, under God, unusual duties and responsibilities. At the same time the depressing effects of Ezra's efforts are clear: the old freedom was gone, for ever. They were now to be *slaves* of Yahweh, in good Semitic fashion, but with a higher, harder, more heroic code than any to be found elsewhere in the ancient world—that is, harder than any other national code.

Obviously, if the Jews were now to be governed by a book containing a detailed code of laws, they must familiarise themselves with its provisions. Hence the synagogue, which, as we have seen, is still primarily the "house of study" of God's Word. One may almost say that it is only incidentally a "house of prayer"—the Old Testament had given this name to the temple (Isa. LVI.7)—or of public worship, or of sacramental ministrations, which among the Jews take place at home. The day of the rabbis was not far distant. The scribes, who were originally the professional copyists of the Law and then its expounders, the leading Schoolmen (the "pairs"), the "men of the great synagogue"—these were now the real teachers of Israel rather than the priests, who had been Israel's teachers in pre-exilic days. Although the term "rabbi" probably comes from the period after the fall of Jerusalem in A.D. 70, when the Jewish schools were reorganised and reopened by the saintly Jochanan ben Zakkai (see p. 22), the *function* of the rabbi, as teacher, scholar, and expounder of scripture, had already been in effect (as George Moore insisted) from the days of Ezra onward, certainly by the time of Ben Sira. The term "teacher of righteousness", used in the Dead Sea Scrolls, is not only perfectly accurate but also very old, perhaps originating before the first or even the second century B.C. It was, of course, no rare and distinguished title, given to only one man in all history, possibly to the founder of the community at Qumrân; nor was it a semi-divine title reserved for the coming Messiah; it was very common—every Jewish community had a "teacher of righteousness", that is, a teacher of *sedakah*, religion.

3. *Methods of Interpretation were Taken Over from Judaism*

It was this idea of scripture as divinely inspired and therefore absolutely authoritative which the church inherited from its Jewish mother-faith. The methods of interpretation, also inherited, were age-old, and included both the literal and the tropological, but not the allegorical: that—as we have seen—was something else, Greek in origin, and the rabbis as a rule did not practise or encourage it. Nor did they make use of the mystical or theosophical method of interpretation; this method they positively discouraged and forbade. But it was assumed that when the same word occurred in two or more verses, some hidden tie or magnetic bond must draw them together, each to throw light upon the other—a very good rule in the study of grammar, diction, syntax, and in philology generally, but not always so useful in theology! Sets of rules, seven in number, or thirteen, or thirty-two, were drawn up by various teachers, by Hillel or Akiba or Ishmael or Eliezer ben Jose ha-Gelili or Philo of Alexandria. Some of these were taken over in the early Christian schools, especially in Alexandria, where Philo's rules and his example led to a great development of allegorical exegesis—for Philo, unlike the rabbis, was an allegorist. In the north, in Syria and Mesopotamia, in Anatolia and Greece and in Italy, at least at first, a more restrained method was observed: the Christian school at Antioch was in close contact with orthodox Jewish scholars and never went the length of allegorism or the theory of multiple meanings in scripture which in time spread over the whole Western church, encouraging the most fantastic feats of exegetical ingenuity, and completely blinding men to the real meaning and purpose of the holy scriptures.[1]

But with the Reformation dawned a new and vital approach to the Bible, a purely religious interpretation made in the light of personal religious experience (chiefly, at first, that of Martin Luther); but also, in consequence, there came a revolt against the arid scholasticism of the preceding centuries with its "fourfold" meaning of scripture, its atomistic theological interpretation, text by text, and its legalistic understanding of the gospel as the *nova lex*. And yet, alas, it was not long before the Reformed theology itself became scholastic, and the "true, literal, historical" meaning of the Bible got confined within a

---

[1] For a fuller account of the history of exegesis see R. M. Grant, *The Bible in the Church* (New York, Macmillan, 1948; revised ed. 1954), and my article "Exegesis" in the new edition of the *Encyclopedia Americana* (both have bibliographies).

M

bibliolatrous "literalism" which has survived to this day, often with bitter controversy and acrimonious name calling. It is a pity that in religion and politics most men are unable to find common ground somewhere between opposing extremes! Either the Bible must be inspired "from cover to cover", including every vowel point, accent, comma, semicolon, and period, or else it is merely "ancient religious literature". Either it contains profound mysteries, to be discerned only by the expert allegorist, or it is a "plain tale" which must come within the comprehension of every village yokel, for whom ancient history, ancient religion, ancient languages, ancient poetry— including the whole environment of holy scripture—simply do not exist.

Is the Bible "true"? Of course! but that does not mean "true" as a timetable is true, or a set of logarithms, or a kitchen recipe, or a text-book in chemistry. One thing our generation greatly needs is a new school of biblical interpreters who will bring out the profound, unchanging, everlasting message of the Bible, its religious and ethical meaning, not the bare bones of literal fact—or presumed fact—about the creation in six days, or the moon standing still in Aijalon, or the mode of Christ's birth, or the empty tomb, or the identity of the "man" described as "number 666", or the events to come in 1290 days or the "time, times, and half a time" of Daniel or Revelation. Neither "literalism" of this kind—it is really "modernism", as Ernest Colwell shows in his *Study of the Bible*—nor allegorism is either needed or useful in the interpretation of scripture. What is really needed is (a) keen intelligence, (b) real learning, the knowledge of history, literature, and philology, (c) religious and moral insight, and (d) the spiritual capacity to hear the voice of God speaking to men today *through* (rather than muffled or smothered within) the Book of books. This is the true Word of God which comes to us even now through the words of holy scripture, as once it came to men of old, but now with a rich meaning and emphasis addressed to our own condition, our own times, our own problems. Religion should not be "interpreted" but transmitted, as Igor Stravinsky has said of music.

We may add that, for a true understanding of the New Testament, a deep and sympathetic understanding of the *Old*

Testament is indispensable. This means more than a knowledge of Hebrew history or the Hebrew language; it involves a religious and poetic understanding of the Hebrew soul, the Hebrew view of life—and also the actual Hebrew *way* of life, as it was lived under the adverse conditions of the ancient Orient, by the inspiration, power, and guidance of the highest and purest religion in that world. And that is to say, guided by the Spirit of God. But it also means a sympathetic, imaginative understanding of ancient literature, especially Oriental. As the late Pope Pius XII insisted, in his famous encyclical on biblical studies, the holy scriptures are full of imagery, and must be interpreted with imagination. Or, as St. Augustine long ago insisted, in his work on the task of Christian teaching, the teacher must begin with a study of "tropes"—figures of speech.[1]

4. *The Problem of Interpretation Today*

There is evidence, we hear, of a widespread revival of interest in the Bible. Whether or not this means a widespread revival of the *study* of the Bible is another question. People speak knowingly of the superiority of the "Judaeo-Christian" or the "biblical" point of view, or they contrast this inheritance with the "Graeco-Roman" or Hellenic, especially as the latter was recovered at the time of the Renaissance. But one sometimes wonders how many of these ardent protagonists of the "biblical" heritage, as superior to the classical, have ever really analysed and compared the two, or have ever read the Plato and Thucydides they glibly condemn. Certainly they have not read the Greek poets—for it seems they never read poetry at all. And both the Bible (the surviving ancient Hebrew literature) and the Greek classics (those that still survive) are mainly poetry. Even the prose of the Bible and the classics is a poetic prose, full of lofty, inspiring imagery, often rhythmic in style, usually correct in choice of words: viewed simply as literature, we cannot spare either the Hebrew or the Greek inheritance. What the advocates of this modern biblicism have in mind, of course, is the out-and-out monotheism of the Bible—as contrasted with pagan literature—and its stern insistence that man is God's creature and therefore

[1] See his *De Doctrina Christiana*, II.16, III.29.

amenable to his laws, that he is helpless in his impotence, both physical and moral, in the sight of God, and that he is therefore wholly dependent upon God for divine grace, forgiveness, spiritual and moral support, and ultimate salvation. But some of these emphases are also found in the literature of Greek religion; and some of them are more clearly stated in Greek than in Hebrew—despite all that is said these days about the limitations of "natural theology". And some of them can never be understood without the clear-sighted analytical-critical method of Greek thought, which was pursued among the Hellenes from the beginning of the sixth century B.C. and onward to the end of ancient civilisation.

The religion of the Bible is ethical monotheism, from beginning to end. The view that Christianity is a "Christo-centric" or "Christological" religion, separate from and only to be contrasted with Judaism, with a new God in place of the old—a view popular fifty years ago—is completely mistaken. So also is the view that Christology is the central emphasis in the early creeds. This view takes it for granted that these creeds—even the early creed-like passages found in the New Testament—were intended to be *summaries* of the Christian faith. But they were not so intended. (1) Even the Apostles' Creed was not meant to summarise the Christian faith, but (like the Thirty-nine Articles and other confessional documents) it was a statement—or a series of statements—on contested points, especially the crucial Gnostic and Docetic perversions of the faith. (2) The total Christian faith, as reflected in the New Testament, is essentially and primarily theistic, that is to say monotheistic, and secondarily Christological. God comes first, as the initiator of revelation, reconciliation, and salvation; he sent his Son, in whom and by whom he was reconciling the world to himself; he raised him from the dead—and so on. (3) Finally, Christ is no mystery deity, in the New Testament, but the prophet and messenger, the agent and representative, the Servant of God or Son of God, entrusted with God's plans and purposes and commissioned to carry them into effect as the fulfiller of the divine will. This conception is basically Semitic, not Greek. It requires for its background a mono-theistic conception of deity—polytheism will not do. The purely Christocentric type of Christianity came later, and it owed far more to Hellenistic-Roman syncretism than to Hebraism, Judaism, the Old Testament—or even the New.

There are statements of Christian teaching which centre in Christology, in the nature of Christ and his work, and at the same time all but ignore theism, the doctrine of the nature, the character and the purposes of God. It is the old Gnosticism all over again, with a difference: God is either the "Great Unknown", the "Veiled Being", as in the ancient *Gnōsis*, or he is simply taken for granted and ignored. There was a time in the history of Protestant dogmatics when the reverse was true: God and his sovereignty, his will and his power, his inscrutable wisdom and providence, were so strongly emphasised that Christ was all but forgotten. But the pendulum has now swung far in the opposite direction, under the influence first of modern romanticism and then of modern humanism or "humanitarianism" and the whole general anthropocentric (as opposed to the ancient theocentric) emphasis in religion and theology. It is impossible to identify this modern humanistic Christology, which has no sound theistic basis, with the teaching of the New Testament. The New Testament never assumes that it is possible to know all about Christ but nothing about God, or to substitute the human-divine Jesus for the Everlasting Father, the Maker of heaven and earth. A generation ago there were ardent enthusiasts who, utterly ignoring the Jewish religion in which Christianity arose and the Greek philosophy to which the early church fathers appealed, vigorously maintained that God is known *only* through Christ, and who consequently did not hesitate to describe the Eternal Creator of the universe as "the Christlike God". There may be those who still repeat this slogan—or who secretly cling to its point of view. I am sure their intentions are good, but their language is most unfortunate. Let us never be misled into thinking that it is the language of the New Testament, which is too thoroughly Jewish and too "biblical" ever to make any such statement as "God is like Christ". Instead, Christ is like God, Christ reveals God, Christ is the one whom God chose and sent and raised from the dead—this is the truly "biblical" language; and it is the language of the early church, the language taken over from Judaism and re-interpreted by identifying Jesus with the coming Messiah.

The enormous present-day emphasis upon Christology, which distorts the true "proportion" of the Faith, and the unquestioning acceptance of Albert Schweitzer's theory of Jesus' "messianic consciousness", interpreted in the light of his further theory that Jesus expected the immediate coming of the Son of Man to hold the Last Judgment, together with the whole airy structure of "thoroughgoing" eschatology including "interim ethics"—all this has characterised much of Protestant theology since 1910. The movement may now be viewed in its true historical perspective. Its real and most important significance is that it continued the huge pendulum-swing away from "Greek metaphysics", begun by Albrecht Ritschl in the two decades preceding Johannes Weiss and Albert Schweitzer. It also repudiated, in principle, the English "Incarnation theology" which had been widely popular in the nineteenth century. But in spite of their declaration of independence and repudiation of Ritschlianism, both Weiss and Schweitzer retained the anti-classical, anti-Hellenic emphasis which characterised that school, only substituting the so-called "messianic consciousness" of Jesus for the super-natural consciousness of the divine Son presupposed in Niceno-Chalcedonian orthodoxy. "Thoroughgoing eschatology" re-pudiated, or at least ignored, the formal Christology of the third, fourth, and fifth centuries, but clung firmly to the *Menschensohndogmatik* of the first century, a dogmatic con-ception which the early church itself soon outgrew and by a complete and diametrically opposed reinterpretation rejected before the first century was over: "Son of God" became Jesus' true title, and expressed his divine nature; "Son of Man" emphasised his lowly humanity—a reinterpretation that, as we have seen, simply exchanged the conceptions which originally belonged to these two terms. This shift took place between the days of Paul and those of Justin Martyr, Irenaeus, and Origen, and its stages are recorded in the short and simple annals of the Monarchians. In fact Paul, who never mentions the term "Son of Man", was probably the one who did most to bring about this change in usage. For him, "the Son of Man" was either an unknown or at least an unused title; his "man from heaven" is not the Enochic "Son of Man" who was with God "before the signs [of the Zodiac] were hung in the sky", but is the "second man", who is the Lord, raised, glorified, and exalted, and destined to judge and rule the whole universe (I Cor. xv.47, Phil. II.10). Paul was not echoing the book of Enoch, any more than he was echoing Philo of Alexandria; he was reflecting upon and expounding the first two chapters of Genesis. By the middle of the second century this shift was more or less complete; no one any longer used the term "Son of Man" in its original apocalyptic-eschatological sense.

Contrasted with all these late nineteenth and early twentieth century "Christological" theories and formulations, the New Testament remains basically Jewish, not Greek—though Greek in language—theistic, not "Christocentric", and it can be understood only from the historical vantage point of the modified Judaism which provided the early church with its terminology and its whole frame of thought.

5. *Modern Biblicism and Dogmatic Theology*

Modern Protestant theology cannot do without a firm biblical foundation for its central doctrines of revelation, grace, and atonement, for much of it now lacks the broader basis of the Incarnation theology which characterised the orthodoxy of the ancient churches. Hence the repudiation of "Greek metaphysics" by Ritschl and his school necessarily involved a retreat to a more purely biblical base, one which, it was thought, would be sufficiently strong to meet the requirements of modern historical and psychological queries and interpretations. The rejection of all views based on the "history of religions" (*Religionsgeschichte*), or even on sound literary, historical, and psychological exegesis of the New Testament, has followed in due course for some of our contemporaries in this field. Like the ancient defences of Syracuse, the outer works were designed not to hold off the enemy but to admit and then destroy him!

But what kind of "biblicism" are we offered as a refuge from modern criticism? There are dogmatic theologians who seem not to have altered their views of New Testament exegesis in fifty years! It is no use telling them that the sentence "God was in Christ" (II Cor. v.19—see pp. xv, 34) is a mistranslation, and that in view of Paul's theology as a whole, and also of his syntax, and the common use made in the New Testament of the suspended participial construction (for example, Rom. 1.20, 1 Cor. xiv.9, Gal. 1.22, Luke 11.33, 111.23, Mark 1.6), it means only, "In Christ, God was reconciling the world to himself"; or that the sentence "Time shall be no more" (Rev. x.6, in the popular hymn version) means only "There will be no further delay", and that it has nothing to do with the medieval or even the Augustinian conception of time and its relation to eternity, and does not justify the useful modern theological phrase "beyond history"; or that the weight of the evidence, based on the author's normal usage, is against *monogenēs theos* ("only begotten God") in John 1.18, and that no counting of hands among ancient manuscripts or copyists will settle it the other way; or that *monogenēs* itself does not mean "only begotten" (which is mere over-translation) but "unique", that is, "only", *unicus* (as in the Vulgate); or that the theory that Jesus was the son of a Galilean village maiden and a German soldier is a contemptible libel, unworthy of any historian's consideration or refutation—and how can any theologian take seriously this ancient slander? He must be very deficient in historical judgment, to consider its incorporation in his system! Too often, the dogmatic theologian has made up his mind long in advance—or has had it made up for him; his convictions are not matters of scholarly judgment at all but are simply *de fide*. If one mentions the problems that confront the critic, he at once loses interest; like Gallio, he "cares for none of these things". All other subjects of study may change and progress, but not textual criticism or exegesis! Is not God's Word eternal and changeless? And if so, must not its interpretation be equally unalterable? One is scarcely surprised to meet with this stubborn objection on the Roman side; but in Protestantism it is truly astonishing—until one reflects that following the repudiation of the ancient classical Christology of Nicaea and Chalcedon, not only of its terminology but also of its modes of thought, and of the whole intellectual process by which the church arrived at the ancient definitions, a theology founded on the Bible can do no other than *freeze* its exegesis at a certain point (say 1880 or 1910) and refuse to admit any change thereafter. It is like establishing a

DEW Line airbase on an ice floe—which must be kept frozen and stable or everything will end in disaster.

Examples of this outmoded conservatism are abundant. Not long ago a religious weekly surveyed the current use of the new *Revised Standard Version* of the Bible in its own denomination and quoted several anonymous criticisms. One was made by a clergyman who resented the failure of the R.S.V. to change the motive of Judas (in Matt. xxvii.3) from repentance to remorse—totally unaware, it would seem, that Matthew's Greek verb describes only the most casual change of mind. Another writer regretted that the new version had failed to distinguish between *phileō* ("like") and *agapaō* ("love") in John xxi.15ff.— as if philologists have not known for fifty years that in Hellenistic Greek this distinction did not hold. Many persons seem to have no conception of the task and duty of a translator, or of the limitations which a scholar's conscience must place upon his freedom in rendering the original. If he is to be a faithful translator, the original meaning of the text, as it was intended by its author and understood by its earliest readers, must be the paramount and controlling consideration. I am reminded of a boy who came to school one day, years ago, when students could still buy the teacher's "answer-book" as well as the pupil's text-book—if they were lucky! This boy brought the wrong book to class. He had all the answers, but had never seen the problems. Similarly, there are those who know what the New Testament ought to say, regardless of the Greek text!

Still another example of this insistence upon an acceptable modern rendering—an example which is the more striking in that it is farther away—is the new South African translation of the Song of Songs. The traditional rendering, "I am black but comely, O ye daughters of Jerusalem", will no longer do, in that land of *Apartheid*. It now reads, "I am comely, and burnt brown by the sun". The real basis of such predilections and preferences is not scholarship at all, but dogmatic theology, dogmatic anthropology, or dogmatic ethics, dictating what scholars ought to find in the Bible, since it is their duty to find support for the tenets of the current dogmatic system. We hear much in these days about the necessity of "demythologising" the New Testament (see p. 33); even more pressing, it seems to me, and even more important than the "deliteralising" mentioned above, is the task of "detheo-logising" the New Testament, and returning it to the church for use in worship, instruction, and personal edification. It is time the New Testament ceased to be subjected to the atom-ising, botanising process which breaks it up into lists of proof texts designed to uphold later systems of dogmatic theology, either medieval or modern. Judaism, happily, has never been overwhelmed by any system of dogmatic theology, and I for one wish the Christian church were equally free from such domination. As Judaism has demonstrated, it is perfectly possible for a religion to live without dogmas, without attempt-ing to define the undefinable.[1]

The consequences of the modern repudiation of "Greek metaphysics", and of classical thought generally in favour of contemporary modes of thought, and also of the rejection of classical literature—poetry, drama, philosophy, and belles-lettres—and even, strangest of all, in view of the history of Protestantism, the neglect of classical *scholarship* in theological education—all this means a profound impoverishment of the human mind and spirit. And yet it is continually promoted by those who discourage theological students who might wish to study Greek, even simple, elementary New Testament Greek, and who urge them instead to spend their time on modern works of philosophy, sociology, and psychology, or even plays and novels—as if a good student could not do both! Thus modern Protestant theology is steadily tending to cut itself adrift from the great tradition of humane studies which has hitherto been central in our Western civilisation, and is seeking

---

[1] According to Anglican theology, there are very few dogmas, i.e. precisely defined, authoritatively decreed definitions of Christian truth which must be accepted by all members of the church. Tradition plays a much larger place in Christian doctrine than most Christians realise. The Anglican theory of con-sensus—a consensus which indeed may conceivably sometime be reversed by ecumenical action (see *Essays Catholic and Critical*, 1926)—seems to be more closely in touch with historical reality than theories which centre either in biblical inerrancy (including inerrant interpretation) or in some living voice or organ entitled to pronounce and to authorise infallible definitions. As Bishop Joseph Hall maintained, in the days of the Westminster Assembly, the most useful of all books of theology would be one with the title, *De paucitate credendorum*, " Of the *fewness* of the articles of faith " which one must accept (see John Morley, *Oliver Cromwell*, 1889, p. 150). As Isaac Casaubon said, in his letter to Cardinal Perrone, *Rex* [James I] *arbitratur, rerum absolutè necessarium ad salutem, non magnum esse numerum.* See also Art. VI of the *Thirty-nine Articles of Religion*.

to compensate for this act of desperation by noisy appeal to "biblical" thought and doctrine, meaning by that the biblicism of the sixteenth and seventeenth centuries, including the exegesis of the age of "Protestant scholasticism". Of course it is far easier simply to accept the authoritative theological exegesis of the sixteenth century, especially when it is set forth in good English translations, than it is to ponder the meaning of hard passages in the Greek New Testament, and then to ransack all ancient literature, papyri, and inscriptions for parallel or similar usages, and finally to face the necessity of making up one's own mind as to the most probable interpretation. Such repudiation of responsibility, and the excuses now offered for doing so, would have seemed, even fifty years ago, not merely disgraceful but even treasonable to the basic principles of the Reformation. For long centuries the dictum "Search the scriptures" was as authoritative a command within historical Protestantism as it was in the early church. But what can these words possibly mean to a minister of today whose teachers have hidden away his tools, or have bidden him not to waste his time in mastering their use, and have supplied him with a collection of cheap, easily-operated, labour-saving gadgets, which will make unnecessary the long, slow, painful intellectual and spiritual toil hitherto required? The answer seems obvious: the command is no longer obeyed. At least one obvious result is the endless, dreary repetition of platitudes and clichés which passes for "biblical" preaching in some pulpits today. The fresh springs of genuine biblical preaching are steadily being choked and filled up with theological rubbish from days long gone by, especially from the dreary scholasticism of that hopelessly desiccated, arid, war-ridden period at the end of the sixteenth and early in the seventeenth centuries. And all this is possible, it seems, largely because in the education of the ministry a narrow professional training, a superficial theological indoctrination, and an interesting "clinical" drill have taken the place of broad preparation in historical and literary studies, in philosophy and classics. We certainly pay dearly for some of our cheap twentieth century "labour-saving" devices, bought on the instalment plan! Much the same can be said of the neglect of the Hebrew language and of ancient Semitic history, civilisation, and religion, above all of ancient Judaism, in the interpretation of the Bible—of the New Testament as well as the Old. Many Christians have not even read the Apocrypha!

Modern research has cast more light upon the Bible, its origin, literary character, and meaning, than upon any other similar body of sacred writings. It has made clear the way in which the Bible Canon came into existence, the stages by which the Old Testament collection grew and was finally authorised at the Jewish Council of Jamnia in A.D. 90, and also the New Testament Canon, which was practically complete by A.D. 180. The Bible was a social possession, both in the synagogue and in the church, and hence was "not of any private interpretation" (II Peter 1.20) nor to be viewed as private property. By its very nature it was the possession of the religious group, and existed for use in public worship and instruction—only secondarily for private study. The use of the Old Testament as a source book for the exposition of the Law (Halakah) came later, among the rabbis. The use of both Testaments as a source for dogmatic and moral theology, presupposing a uniform, consistent "biblical" theology from cover to cover, came later still, among the church fathers, the Schoolmen, the early Protestant theologians and system builders. It was of course viewed as inspired, and therefore sacred and authoritative. It was the record of a divine revelation, from Moses—or the Creation—onward. Hence the easy step to a consistent, uniform "theology" embracing the whole—in an age when a theological system was the chief religious desideratum, or when warring sects all made their ultimate appeal to the inspired words of scripture.

But the unfortunate consequences of this view are now becoming clearer every day. Antiquated exegesis and historical interpretation survive under the aegis of a revived "biblical" orthodoxy, and threaten to stifle and destroy the freedom of Protestant scholarship. The same ultra-conservatism also keeps alive the anti-Judaism at the heart of certain traditional Protestant theologies, and it does so by falsely claiming to be "biblical"—as if the whole Old Testament and also all of the New, except for two epistles, went into the discard, and only Romans and Galatians set forth the truly "biblical" teaching! This reactionary theology is a centre of anti-Judaism—as a

natural consequence of its requirement of logical consistency
in a theological system based upon the Bible, and its frequent
devotion to apocalyptic and millennarian "prophecy".   The
practical consequences are obvious.   Much of the recent
violence in the United States, for example, including the
profanation or destruction of Jewish synagogues, has taken
place in the "Bible Belt", where "biblical" orthodoxy is
common and indigenous.   Elsewhere this "biblical" orthodoxy
is the stronghold of reactionary "racism", as in the Reformed
Dutch Church in South Africa.   Judaism, fortunately, is free
from the dominance of ancient dogmatic systems;   and the
Bible will not come into its own, and speak its full message, we
believe, until Protestantism claims and achieves complete
freedom for historical interpretation.   At the same time, the
church cannot safely abandon either its Jewish or its classical
heritage—both are priceless, irreplaceable, and indispensable
for a true understanding and interpretation of holy scripture.

CHAPTER ELEVEN

Dogma and Ethics

In addition to the theological dogmas already described, there are certain popular dogmas which make a sound and true historical interpretation of the Bible impossible. They also have a bearing upon the attitude of many persons toward ancient Judaism. Every one of them is related, directly or indirectly, to the anti-Jewish prejudice which still plagues and distorts much of our interpretation of holy scripture. The extent to which these popular dogmas interfere with and really prevent a fair understanding of the Bible is not commonly realised; but a teacher soon discovers the strength of the opposition to serious historical study. This phenomenon is not limited to the study of the sacred scriptures, of course; there is a widespread unconcern for everything that involves the past. For our generation, the pert declaration on a federal building in Washington is characteristic: "The past is prologue"—with no apologies to Shakespeare! This jejune dictum is only one remove from Henry Ford's silly remark, "History is bunk", or Carl Sandburg's "The past is a bucket of ashes". To the interpreter of the Bible, this growing contempt for the past is a tragically serious omen.

1. *Dogmas That Prevent Sound Interpretation*

One of these dogmas (*a*) is the widespread notion that ancient Judaism was a "bookkeeping" religion, devoted exclusively to the establishment of personal merit and credit with God. But this is untrue—look at the religion reflected in the Psalms, the Shemoneh Esreh, the Pirqe Aboth (see 1.3!),

or the books now contained in the Apocrypha and Pseudepi-
grapha, or the oldest Pharisaic traditions.

Another (*b*) is the idea that the Old Testament was wholly
concerned with the doctrine of the Covenant and the New
Testament with *Heilsgeschichte*, that is, the rejection of Israel
and the abrogation of the Mosaic Law, making way for the
spread of the gospel. Both ideas are more modern than
ancient. Certainly their almost mathematical formulation is
very recent. Would anyone seriously consider taking *Heilsgeschichte* for a sound formula in interpreting *political* history?
Yet if it is true at all it must embrace political history, since
for the ancient world there was no sharp distinction between
politics and religion: God, or the gods, were concerned with
both. Religion was half politics, since it concerned the
survival, welfare, or triumph of the state—which was a religious
institution, with sacred sanctions, legends, functions, and
purposes. The theory is doubtless due to an exclusive and
one-sided concentration upon certain isolated passages in the
Bible, for example the fiery apocalyptic announcement of the
penalty to be paid by one generation for all the blood shed upon
earth since the creation of the world; or Paul's morose con-
templation of the strange rejection of Christ by his own people,
and the problem of Israel's ultimate salvation. It is a theory
derived from isolated utterances which come from a time of
acute depression and despair, the period just preceding the
inevitable doom of the Jewish state; it is certainly not a fair
presentation of the total Hebrew-Jewish-Christian outlook
upon world history. It is no more typical or representative of
the biblical view than Herodotus' theory of the envy of
the gods was typical of Greek thought: it fitted his own time
like a glove, when the collapse of the old Oriental empires,
and now the repulse of Persia and the heroic but temporary
unification of Greek defence let one believe that great empires
always run their course and eventually fall. But could the
theory have been maintained in the century following, when
a mania of independence and rivalry had overtaken the
Greeks themselves and was leading to national suicide? Nations
are really self-destroyed, not smitten down by the gods. And
a theory whose falsity is proved by political history can hardly
be proved true by religious.

Every doctrine must be tested by what it does to the central doctrine of all, the doctrine of God. If the theory of *Heilsgeschichte* represents God as a sentimental aged *Shayik* with favourites among his children, who eventually becomes alienated by their unfilial behaviour, and who accepts the devotion of others only as a substitute for what he has failed to receive from his own—all this must be rejected as unworthy of "the God and Father of our Lord Jesus Christ", however well it may once have suited the mood or explained the condition of those who thus recognised (1) the prior claims and prerogatives of the Jewish people and also the undeniable, irrefutable fact of (2) Israel's almost total "rejection" of the new messianic gospel of salvation and (3) the unquestionable divine acceptance of penitent Gentiles.

Still another popular dogma in "biblical" interpretation (c) is the "existentialist" theory that the first question, rather than the last, should always be, "What does this passage mean to *me*?"—a question which takes precedence over all the facts in the case, historical, philological, or literary. This is the simplest kind of biblicism, and really goes back to the days of Pietism. Noble as have been many of the advocates of this view, its ultimate bearings are quite unreliable and often lead to the total distortion of the meaning of holy scripture.

Still another dogma, one which we often hear invoked, (d) assumes that exegesis is the result of personal predilection on the part of exegetes: for example, once more, the committee which produced the new *Revised Standard Version* of the Bible were all "liberals" and so produced a "liberal" version, or —*mirabile dictu*—they were mostly fundamentalists, and therefore produced a fundamentalist version. This strange prejudice even arises in churches traditionally liberal in theology. By all the tokens of intellectual and doctrinal ancestry, they should still be free from personal predilections in exegesis, devoted to sound interpretation, take account of the views of the church as a whole, and maintain them in proper balance! But the current neo-"biblicism", like much of modern thought in other areas, is sicklied o'er with the pale cast of subjectivism, self-analysis, introspection; and the assumption that scholarship must likewise be subjective is only a further projection of this strange state of mind.

Finally, (e) there is the widespread neglect of New Testament ethics—or even, on the part of some persons, aversion for "mere" ethics in general and therefore for the ethics of the New Testament. They are viewed either as utterly Utopian and idealistic, impossible of observance in practice, and designed only to convince men of their helpless, hopeless impotence, and thus to compel them to throw themselves upon God's mercy, relying solely upon divine forgiveness, justification, and grace; or else, on the other hand, as tame, pedestrian, "Jewish" morals, so that anyone who tries to observe them is sure to fall into dull, complacent "moralism" and self-justification—as if mere observance of the Ten Commandments had something to do with salvation! But, we recall, that is precisely what Jesus taught (Mark x.17-22).

2. *The New Testament Ethics*

At first glance, it is true, Christian ethics—especially as set forth in the Gospel of Matthew—look like a purely accidental combination of heterogeneous elements, Jewish legalism, Christian spirituality, asceticism, even stray echoes of Cynicism, especially in the Sermon on the Mount. Some passages belong to early Canon Law, with its prudential tempering of Jesus' out-and-out eschatological teaching—for example, the admonition to use foresight in litigation (Matt. v.25f.; contrast Luke XII.57ff.), the prohibition of oaths (Matt. v.33-37), or the modification of his prohibition of remarriage after divorce (Matt.v.32, XIX.9). This of course does not deny that Christian ethics, as set forth in the New Testament, may be the highest hitherto attained, or even the final code for all mankind. But the heterogeneity is clear.

Yet the whole point of Christian ethics, at least as set forth in the New Testament, is that they are not really "ethics" (*ēthika*) at all, but the "righteousness" which God requires in those who are to enter his Kingdom—a righteousness based upon both the "essential" nature of man, as Paul Tillich insists, and the "pure" will of God, as Martin Dibelius held. That is to say, they are purely and simply a *religious* ethics, and cannot be fitted into any other system, even as its crown and climax, or established upon any other foundation than the Jewish or early Christian conception of the coming Reign of God, the

N

eschatological conception and world view. Jesus' teaching presupposed the religious teaching of the Old Testament and Judaism, save where he explicitly corrected or modified it. He showed its further practical application, brought out its deepest and most fundamental implications and presuppositions, as in his teaching on marriage, oaths, vows, and the "pious works" of prayer, fasting, and almsgiving; and he deepened and "fulfilled" its moral range and consequences. This the other Jewish teachers likewise did—not so much the ordinary scribes, with their concern for details of casuistry in daily life, as the great teachers and heads of schools, who dealt with the far-reaching implications of the divine Law: Maimonides, for example, who showed that the manufacture of weapons for export and international sale was contrary to the Torah (see his *Mishneh Torah*, 1.77a). The armourer's trade promoted wars and provided Israel's enemies with the means of attack! The few brief counsels contained in the gospels cannot possibly be viewed either as a system of ethics or as a complete guide to religious conduct, save as expressing principles which must be formulated and applied in harmony with these precepts. Joseph Klausner complains that Jesus has nothing to say to the judge on the bench. But did Jesus *intend* to say anything (Luke XII.14)? Or did he assume a position from which it was to be expected that he would issue such counsel? His teaching presupposed the whole of Judaism except in so far as he corrected or altered it, chiefly by way of emphasis. This is always the way of the prophet and reformer —who come "not to destroy but to fulfill".

It is the separation of Christian ethics from their natural background in the Old Testament, their true realm of presuppositions in ancient Judaism, which has done the greatest harm to their interpretation at the present time. We hear—as we have just noted—that the gospel ethics were intentionally set forth in impossible terms, in order to throw men back upon the grace and forgiveness of God—a view somewhat like Paul's artificial conception of the Law as designed to "bring out" sin, and to make men aware of it. Or we hear that the Sermon on the Mount was concerned only with "the pure will of God"—as Dibelius held—regardless of consequences, and without considering whether or not men *could* do the will of God and meet his requirements. All this is true, no doubt, naïve as it may sound, but the simple fact is that Jesus never stopped to consider whether or not his "ethics" were "practicable". Neither did the ancient teachers of Israel ponder the question of practicability, as we may infer from the ethical sections in such books as I and II Enoch, the Testaments of the Twelve Patriarchs, and other sources. We do not refer to the pedestrian, this-worldly ethics of the Wisdom teachers, like Sirach, nor to the expositions of the sacred Law by the Tannaim, the preachers, or the later Talmudists—obviously the Law *was* practicable and they were dealing with cases. But the flaming devotees, the teachers of an ethics based on the command to "love the Lord thy God with all thy heart, and thy neighbour as thyself", those for whom the Reign of God was their dearest desire in life—these men went far beyond the careful calculations of "the little less and the little more", and swept the whole of human obligation into one all-inclusive devotion. "Render to Caesar what is his"—it is not much! "Render to God what is his"—the whole of life! (Mark XII.17). Jesus spoke their language and they his. Hair-splitting theological distinctions, or moralistic, casuistic definitions of precisely how little or how much is required, can never reach the depths of this profound religious ethic. For it is grounded in the total relation of men to God, the total consecration of one's being and existence to him, the total response of loyalty and love on the part of God for his people, his children, his saints, his "poor"—as in the Psalms. And it is out of this religious atmosphere that the gospel ethics arose. We make a grave mistake if we try to interpret them in any other way, as prudential, social-economic, political, Marxist, scientific, or philosophical. They are the flaming proclamation of an utter devotion to God, an utter consecration to his purposes, and "ethics" is really an inadequate, even a misleading term to use. In the hour of crisis, then striking for all mankind, what else could men ask but what God required of them? What else could they do but undertake to meet it? Perhaps we too shall discover, someday, that for us also there is no alternative: for we too may face the final crisis, the end of our world, the total destruction of this old order with its compromises, its complacencies and halfway measures, its lip service to God but real devotion to mammon.

N 2

It will not be ethics that will save us, not even the "ethics" of the gospel, but only God in his mercy. Then only those will be saved who turn to him with all their hearts, not counting the cost, and not pausing to consider the possibility of doing his perfect will.

3. *The Agrarian Protest*

In a book on New Testament thought[1] I once described "the agrarian protest" as part of the background of New Testament ethics. At least one reviewer found the chapter unconvincing. Perhaps so; but the argument requires a clear view of the distant background, one that is longer even than the thousand years covered by biblical literature, and broader. For the evidence is drawn from the whole of ancient Mediterranean history.

(1) In Hebrew life and thought there had been for hundreds of years a steady and repeated protest against the settled life of Canaan and the crowded life of cities. The Rechabites, for example (Jer. xxxv), looked back with nostalgic longing to the free life of the desert, and constantly reminded their hearers that Jacob had once "dwelt in tents". The vine was the symbol of the settled agricultural economy of Palestine, in contrast with that of the desert; from its product, wine, they totally abstained. The prophets likewise looked back to the wilderness-wandering as a time when Canaanite customs were unknown, including even the rites of animal sacrifice. But as time went on, the settled economy of Israel triumphed, and the old nomadic ideal grew dim. Instead of a protest against settled agricultural life in favour of the freedom of the wilderness, protest was now made against urban life, in favour of the country. Many scattered traces of this protest are to be found here and there in the Old Testament, but chiefly they appear in the apocryphal and apocalyptic literature (for example, 1 Enoch).[2]

(2) A similar process of change in outlook also took place in Greek and Roman social thinking. By the fifth century B.C.

---

[1] *An Introduction to New Testament Thought*, pp. 303ff.

[2] See my articles on "The Economic Significance of Messianism", in the *Anglican Theological Review*, VI.196-213; VII.281-289; and "Economic Messianism and the Teaching of Jesus", *ib.*, XII.443-447.

the Greek *polis* was the centre of Greek civilisation; but with the decline of the *polis* in religious and political importance during the following century, and especially after Alexander's conquest of the Persian Empire, men became aware of the advantages of the country over the town. Under Augustus, the trend toward country life was in full swing. Some of this idealisation of rural life was excessive—it even went the length of making out the barbarians of the northern forests to be a race superior to the old and effete city dwellers in Mediterranean lands. But not all was exaggeration: the pictures of country life sketched by Theocritus, Virgil, Horace, even Lucretius and Ovid—not to mention Tacitus—are most attractive, even charming, and doubtless true. But there was also protest. The wealth of the city was a constant provocation to resentment by the hard-working tillers of the soil, upon whom the burdens of manual labour—with crude tools or none—the adverse economic conditions of their lot, and the political injustices of the age bore most heavily. Simultaneously with the delightful "praises of country life" were voiced the bitter, age-old protests against extortion and oppression, protests as old as Hesiod and the Egyptian tale of the *Complaints of the Peasant*.[1]

(3) Now it is against the background of this ancient agrarian or peasant outlook on life that the gospel ethics must be studied—a "wisdom" so old that it is found throughout the Near East and in Egypt, centuries before the Old Testament was written. In such a world, going the second mile, giving to anyone who begs, not letting your left hand know what your right hand does, speaking the simple truth, caring for the sick, the poor, and the helpless, even mourning or burying their dead, not resisting the "evil" man, the aggressor, not returning evil for evil or reviling for reviling—these were the commonplaces of gnomic wisdom, set forth in many proverbs and "sayings of the wise"; and in such a world Jesus' ethics were relevant and full of meaning, and were at once recognised as true and binding. Celsus and Nietzsche were half-right: Christianity really is an ethic for slaves; only, it was meant, in the first instance, for peasants, the poor and humble, dwelling in the country or in small towns, not for proletarian

---

[1] On ancient Greek and Roman agriculture, W. E. Heitland's *Agricola*, (Cambridge, 1921) still provides a valuable survey.

mobs. The early Christian sharing of property (Acts 11.44f.) was a perfectly natural procedure in a pioneer enclave or colony of rural peasants living in a big city. It was by no means an example of "communism", or even of "socialism", for it lacked both basic theory and compulsion.

The conception of "good old days" appealed to many persons—in Greek and Roman circles as well as in Hebrew and Jewish. The nomadic past—or the rural—was idealised, and even primitive life was painted in glowing colours by the Roman poets. In Palestine, in the time of Jesus, "No king but God!" was the Zealot slogan; but it appealed to many others in addition to the fanatical revolutionists. It is even echoed in the Shemoneh Esreh—as we have seen (see p. 47). For it not only presupposed the theocratic society envisaged in the Torah, especially as it was interpreted and applied under the Second Commonwealth, but it also took for granted the rule of perfect justice in an agrarian society organised under the divine sovereignty. "God made the country, man the town." So also in the gospels: if the motive of their "ethics" is the pure will of God, nevertheless, the language, the medium in which they are conceived and expressed belongs to the country, to Galilee, the land of farmers and fishermen, builders and small tradesmen, not the great imperial city with its sharp contrasts of opulence and poverty, its cruel, heartless inability even to understand the peasant and his problems. Once more, the ancient Jewish, agrarian, Galilean background of the gospel is both clearly implied and indispensable for its true interpretation. But this does not limit or confine its application. The agrarian background of much of the early rabbinic teaching also deserves study: the language, the illustrations, parables, and social presuppositions alike reflect, in many instances, the rural or small town situation and its problems—even though Pharisaism, as Louis Finkelstein has shown, was urban, on the whole, not rural, in its origins and customary setting.

4. *The Need for a New Liberalism*

This soundly historical approach to the New Testament and its ethics was just beginning to gain ground fifty years ago, but it never got very far. The so-called "social gospel", now widely rejected, and even ridiculed, was not its only, or its best, representative. The rejection of this "social gospel" has carried with it the rejection of a truer appraisal of Jesus' ethics than any of the interpretations set forth in its place.

But where are the liberals of yesteryear? They are needed now! Another theology is becoming dominant in Protestant circles; it has taken the place of our traditional Anglo-Saxon liberalism, and its advocates have persuaded the present generation that nineteenth century liberalism was a betrayal of Christianity. But the new orthodoxy, now advancing and eager to gain control of all modern religious thought, turns out to be both agnostic and amoral: agnostic, since God is unknown, and really cannot be known; amoral, since it has little to say about duty but much about sin, and condemns moral instruction as tending to "mere moralism" or "mere Judaism" —as if the Ten Commandments were out of date. But the crisis of today, which involves both faith and morals, calls for a renewal of positive faith and definite teaching of religion and morals. And the only way in which these can now be taught effectively is upon a liberal historical-traditional view, one which is in contact with the great human past, and yet seeks to "bring forth out of its treasure things new and old" (cf. Matt. XIII.52). Far from the liberal view of the Bible being antiquated or outmoded, it is the point of view from which biblical teaching is most sorely needed at the present day.

One sometimes wonders how it was ever possible, after the great advance in the historical study of the Bible which was achieved in Great Britain and America as well as on the Continent between 1890 and 1930, for the current quasi-fundamentalist reaction to take place, and for appeal to the letter of scripture and to dogmatic authority in its interpretation to be reinstated once more, at least over wide areas of contemporary thought. But the explanation is obvious: many large groups, and also many influential leaders, who had subscribed, more or less, to critical views in the early 1920's were never really or deeply convinced of either their truth or their importance for religious thought. At the same time many large religious blocs were never even favourably disposed toward criticism—especially the Roman Catholic church and the more conservative Protestant bodies, together with most

Orthodox Jews. Finally, the diversity of religious interests among Protestants, and even among Catholics, weakened the adherence of many to critical views. How could we have expected anything else? Those for whom religion means chiefly an enthusiasm for social welfare, or the intense pursuit of personal piety and the spiritual life, or the correct performance of liturgical worship and the administration of the sacraments, or the working out of a practical Christian ethic and moral theology, or the promotion of church unity, or the cultivation and advancement of the church's fine arts—architecture, music, vestments—or an advancing missionary campaign at home and abroad, or an intense programme of "soul-winning" —how could such persons be expected to be interested in the detailed literary and historical study of the Bible? Indeed, why *should* they be interested? For at least 90 per cent. of Christian people, Christian theology, worship, customs, literature, and standards of behaviour are not subjects of research but expressions of an art, a way of life; and this is what religion always has been, what religion really is. Those persons who care seriously and with conviction, with total self-committal, about historical and literary criticism, or those who care deeply about the past, are in a very small minority, compared with the great majority of religious men and women, for whom religion is chiefly a matter of present activity, experience, and hope.

5. *The True Use of the Bible*

What then is the true use of the Bible, our greatest inheritance from Judaism? Clearly its function is religious, as it has been ever since the scriptures were first collected to form a Canon—or two Canons, the Jewish and the Christian. It was not for the purpose of providing a body of source material for the study of the history of the Hebrew religion, the Jewish, or the early Christian—as one might have supposed fifty years ago. Nor, at the opposite extreme, was it in order to provide source material for dogmatic theology, or a basis for the construction of theological systems—as one might have supposed in the fourth or fifth century, when the theologising process was in full swing, or in the thirteenth, when it reached its climax in Scholasticism, or in the sixteenth, when its final

Roman Catholic formulation was achieved at the Council of Trent, or in the seventeenth, when Protestant Scholasticism reached its final development. Neither of these two extremes, historicism or dogmatism, provides the answer. Something more central, and in closer accord with the original purpose of the two collections, must be found.

The central and most essential function of the scriptures in the Christian church is still, as in ancient Judaism, the liturgical. Of course, we must give the word its full meaning, which goes far beyond "ritual and ceremony" or the mere formality of public worship. The Bible is the guide and provides the norm for the prayer life of the Christian community. It is the great treasury of historical recollection which gives meaning to the festivals at which the Christian church celebrates the crucial, unrepeatable, classical moments of its creation, expansion, and survival. Like the Passover *seder* in the liturgical life of Judaism, the story which explains and gives its fullest meaning to the observance (see Exodus XII), the passages from the gospels likewise keep alive the meaning of the church's origin and earliest history, centring in the story of the Passion, the Resurrection, and Pentecost. This is, of course, *not* theology. For theology is a purely intellectual construction, impossible without some degree of external stimulus, coming from outside itself, that is, from philosophy—like the grain of sand in the oyster. Instead, the reading of the Bible is the expression of the deepest and holiest life of the church itself, its life with God: not of the individual in his solitariness, his separation from everyone else, but of the holy community, which includes and embraces him in its life-giving warmth and vitality, guided by the Holy Spirit, nourished by divine grace.

From the beginning, the Bible has always been primarily a liturgical work, the holy book read, studied, expounded, pondered, memorised, and accepted by the worshipping congregation as its indispensable guide for living. It was not a collection of oracles, meant to be analysed, taken apart, and then put together again in a new order—as in the old-fashioned systematic catalogues of texts, for example, Roswell Dwight Hitchcock's *Complete Analysis of the Holy Bible, or the Old and New Testament Arranged According to Subjects in 27 Books* (1870) or John Henry Pinnock's *Analysis of Holy Scripture* (1871)—to name only two of the books on "Scripture Harmonised" that fill the shelves of old libraries and represent the theological activity of many minds during the last third of the nine-teenth century. For most Christians, the Bible is simply the church's book, used at public worship and in religious in-struction; this was true long before the theologians took it over, and it is still true, regardless of theological theories.

Theology is of course inevitable, and has its proper place in relation to biblical studies—though this place also, as many now believe, is subsidiary to the liturgical use of the scriptures. But theology should take for granted only genuinely historical, soundly philological, positively religious exegesis.   In our exegesis we are not annotating Cicero's letters but Paul's, not the works of Herodotus or Tacitus but the gospels. But at the very least our standard should be as high as the one required in the exposition of the "secular" classics! And our theology should be genuinely religious. The irreligious exegete, or the undevout systematic theologian, will probably miss the very heart of the matter. Of course the undevout exegete or philologist will probably make some headway—his purpose is scientific and objective; whereas the undevout theologian is simply hopeless, and so is the unhistorical theological interpreter of the Bible, who reads into it whatever he chooses.   Let biblical theology flourish and abound!   But let it be truly biblical, not an intrusion of dogmatics into the interpretation of holy scripture, and let it be truly historical, not intuitive or individualistic or metaphysical!

Finally, the use of the Bible in personal devotion and in religious education is likewise subsidiary to its use in public worship. Yet the three are really one, and the place of worship in religious education is far more important than has usually been assumed. In all three the use must be selective. We should choose only those passages that are truly relevant, truly religious, truly inspired and therefore inspiring. This is no easy assignment; but the task of the religious teacher has always included responsibility for "rightly handling the word of truth" (II Tim. II.15). Accordingly, the true attitude to the scriptures, and their proper use, is the one which explains their first collection, in ancient Judaism and in the early Christian church. It is the liturgical use, central to all the purposes of worship and study, and normative for the religious life in all its aspects—not only for theology, not only for education, not only for private devotion, but for the whole way of living within the religious group.

6. *The Present Task*

The crisis now confronting the world results from the breakdown not only of religion but of morals—traditionally and historically the two have gone together. There is enough "dynamite" in the language of the Bible to blow society to atoms—as the poet Lowell once remarked; and as King Robert of Sicily long ago observed of the *Magnificat*,

> 'Tis well that such seditious words are sung
> Only by priests and in the Latin tongue
>
> (Longfellow, *The Sicilian's Tale*).

But this energy may be harnessed and converted to constructive uses, like the atomic energy which can either annihilate or benefit mankind. Unfortunately, our religious groups cannot even co-operate, let alone unite, even when faced by forces which threaten us with destruction. One might expect religion to unite men, but it has hitherto proved to be one of the most divisive forces in human society. Certain basic convictions stand in the way of religious unity, for example, that of a "true" religion in comparison with which all others are "false"; or that of a "true" church which is entitled to ostracise and ignore all others; or that of a single infallible definition of orthodox belief to which all others must be conformed; or that of one and only one authoritative interpretation of holy scripture. The major divisions of the Christian church, between East and West, between Rome and Protestantism, between Evangelical, Reformed, and all other types of Protestantism, between Conservative, Orthodox, Fundamentalist, Neo-orthodox, and Liberal Christians—all this unbelievable proliferation of conflict, competition, and unending "dissidence of dissent" has effectually prevented the church from bringing to bear its full influence upon the modern world. In theory, its reserve force is incalculable, and might, if clearly articulated and practically applied, save the world from itself and stay its further steps toward degeneration and ultimate suicide. Closely

allied with the church, the Jewish forces should be included—
certainly in America and in Great Britain, where Jews are
often in the forefront of charitable, "social", and "humani-
tarian" movements. Furthermore, the world over, there are
many others who would rally to a united religious front if it
were dedicated to the total betterment of mankind here and
now—not merely to its improved economic status or welfare.
Many Buddhists, many Muslims, many in other religions, and
some with no articulate religion at all might join such a movement, if only Christians and Jews would take the initiative.
This is no merely private speculation by a historian, as some
affirm; for Arnold Toynbee's brilliant argument is supported
by many personal contacts and conversations, public and
private—for example, those of Miss Marian Anderson during
her well-known visit to the Far East.

But the churches, at least officially, are not yet troubled by
their own impotence, triviality, and ineffectiveness, or by the
failure of Christianity to change moral and social conditions
all about them. Indeed, the sectarian and theological trans-
formation of the Christian religion has gone so far that some
groups even oppose all attempts to bring about "social reform"
or "human betterment" as interfering with the church's
commission to preach the message of salvation and grace! The
teaching of morals, or the study and teaching of moral theology,
is discouraged as tending toward "moralism" and self-
righteousness. As a consequence, millions of children grow
up with no positive moral teaching whatsoever. The family
has widely broken down as an institution for inculcating moral
standards—children are supposed to grow up "naturally" and
"unrepressed". In America the schools are forbidden to teach
morals—since Protestants will not accept Catholics as teachers,
nor Catholics accept Protestants. The result is often moral
chaos; we call it "juvenile delinquency", but it is obviously
the result of adult irresponsibility and lowering of standards.

Is it any wonder if without teaching, training, and discipline
in the home or in the school the child never matures, never
achieves *self*-discipline—the only kind of discipline that really
counts, without which moral character is impossible? Or that
he never arrives at moral convictions of his own, and cannot
be expected to resist strong temptations in later life, whether

in public office or in private acts, whether financial or legal, as in the purchase or sale of influence, the winning of political support, the handling of entrusted funds, the advertising of products, the treatment of competitors, the public, or his own employees—or any of the multitude of moral crevices that exist in our modern social structure? (We do not mention outright gangsterism and crime.) The weak ones who yield are still a minority, we are told. But how long will this remain true, if nothing is done to inculcate moral standards, moral principles, moral tests, either in home, school, or church? If the argument of this book is sound, there is every reason for Christians and Jews to affiliate and work loyally together for the establishment of higher and better standards of public education. This new and better education should include not only the teaching of the traditional three "r's" (reading, writing, and arithmetic), but also the indispensable fourth—*righteousness*. For without righteousness, as both the Old Testament and the New affirm, nations perish, and the life of individuals ends in futility, frustration, and emptiness.

What might our world be like if only our religious forces would unite, wherever unity is feasible, or would at least co-operate more closely, where actual unity is still impossible! At last we might begin to see the fulfilment of the ancient promises—

> For the earth shall be full of the knowledge of the Lord
> As the waters cover the sea (Isa. xi.9),

even as the Hebrew prophet foretold. Or, as the ancient Christian apocalyptist sang, in confident anticipation,

> The kingdom of the world has become the Kingdom of our Lord
> And of his Anointed (Rev. xi.15).

As a beginning, I would suggest that Jews might now and then include the Lord's Prayer in their devotions. To say the least, it is one of the most beautiful, most searching, most comprehensive of all Jewish prayers, closely similar to the glorious phrases of the Shemoneh Esreh and the ancient Kaddish. And I wish that Christians would occasionally say the Shema with its accompanying prayers, or use the ancient

Jewish grace at meals, or offer the sublime prayer of the Jewish wife and mother as she lights the Sabbath lamp. I myself have conducted Christian services which included the Shemoneh Esreh, and have found that it was full of meaning to the congregation. Such practices would be only a beginning, but they might eventually lead much farther—not to the conversion of Jews to Christianity, which I am not urging—I wish we might give up all "missions to Jews" and begin to understand one another; or the conversion of Christians to Judaism, though I would gladly see far more men and women converted to the imperishable heart of the Jewish faith, its utter trust in God, its utter devotion to his revealed will. They might even lead, eventually, to a revival of religious faith and a deepening of moral conviction, by which our world could be led out of its present chaos—a condition produced by the unbridled ambition, greed, and self-seeking of modern man, unguided and undeterred by religious or moral considerations, and following only the dim light of his own completely amoral "modern science"—and what he takes to be its social and personal implications. It would not necessarily lead to the Kingdom of God; but at least our faces might be turned in that direction once more.

Index

1. Persons

2. Subjects

PRINTED IN GREAT BRITAIN BY OLIVER AND BOYD LTD., EDINBURGH